Exploring Advanced Features in C#

Enhance Your Code and Productivity

Dirk Strauss

Apress®

Exploring Advanced Features in C#: Enhance Your Code and Productivity

Dirk Strauss
Uitenhage, South Africa

ISBN-13 (pbk): 978-1-4842-4855-3 ISBN-13 (electronic): 978-1-4842-4856-0
https://doi.org/10.1007/978-1-4842-4856-0

Managing Director, Apress Media LLC: Welmoed Spahr
Acquisitions Editor: Smriti Srivastava
Development Editor: Matthew Moodie
Coordinating Editor: Shrikant Vishwakarma

Cover designed by eStudioCalamar

Cover image designed by Freepik (www.freepik.com)

Distributed to the book trade worldwide by Springer Science+Business Media New York, 233 Spring Street, 6th Floor, New York, NY 10013. Phone 1-800-SPRINGER, fax (201) 348-4505, e-mail orders-ny@springer-sbm.com, or visit www.springeronline.com. Apress Media, LLC is a California LLC and the sole member (owner) is Springer Science + Business Media Finance Inc (SSBM Finance Inc). SSBM Finance Inc is a **Delaware** corporation.

For information on translations, please e-mail rights@apress.com, or visit http://www.apress.com/rights-permissions.

Apress titles may be purchased in bulk for academic, corporate, or promotional use. eBook versions and licenses are also available for most titles. For more information, reference our Print and eBook Bulk Sales web page at http://www.apress.com/bulk-sales.

Any source code or other supplementary material referenced by the author in this book is available to readers on GitHub via the book's product page, located at www.apress.com/978-1-4842-4855-3. For more detailed information, please visit http://www.apress.com/source-code.

Printed on acid-free paper

I would like to dedicate this book to my wife Adele and my children Tristan and Irénéé. Thank you for all your support and love. You guys complete me and give me a reason to do what I do. I love you forever and a day.

Table of Contents

About the Author

**Dirk Strauss** is a software developer and Microsoft .NET MVP from South Africa with over 13 years of programming experience. He has extensive experience in SYSPRO Customization (an ERP system), with C# and web development being his main focus. He currently works as a full stack developer with Embrace. He studied at Nelson Mandela University where he wrote software part time to gain a better understanding of the technology. He remains passionate about writing code and imparting what he learns with others.

About the Technical Reviewer

James McCaffrey works for Microsoft Research in Redmond, Wash. James has a PhD in cognitive psychology and computational statistics from the University of Southern California, a BA in psychology, a BA in applied mathematics, and an MS in computer science. He worked on several key products including Azure and Bing. He is also the Senior Technical Editor for Microsoft's *MSDN Magazine*, the most widely read technical journal in the world.

Acknowledgments

I would like to thank the team at Apress for their dedication to this book and for giving me the opportunity to write it.

I would also like to thank James McCaffrey for checking that I had dotted all the i's, crossed all the t's, and that the code made sense. It is always a pleasure working with you.

Lastly, I would like to thank Dave Long for his guidance and mentorship. You have a true passion for your art that inspires me to be a better developer. Kudos mate.

Introduction

This book is primarily aimed at C# developers with some prior knowledge of writing applications in C# with Visual Studio. It is focused on C# 7 but also takes a look at the new features in C# 8 and .NET Core 3.0. In this book, we will

- Look at features of C# 7 such as tuples, local functions, and discards

- Explore abstract classes, implementing interfaces, using async and await, nullable, and dynamic types

- Look at features of C# 8 such as nullable reference types, recursive patterns, ranges, indices, switch expressions, and more

- Create responsive web apps using ASP.NET MVC. Using SASS, jQuery, creating Models, Views, and Controllers. How to use Razor, adding plugins, testing responsive layouts using Chrome, and debugging jQuery using Chrome Developer Tools

- See what is new in .NET Core 3.0 and how to get up and running with .NET Core 3.0 in a Snap

- Have a look at running your ASP.NET Core MVC app on Linux and how to edit and debug it using Visual Studio Code

- Look at new features in Visual Studio 2019

- See how Visual Studio Live Share works

- Learn some refactoring and code fix tips in Visual Studio to make you more productive

- See how you can bring Artificial Intelligence to Visual Studio by making use of the powerful Visual Studio IntelliCode

If you are a developer that wants to keep on improving your skills, have a look at what this book has to offer.

CHAPTER 1

C# 7 in Focus

C# 7 was released in March 2017 as part of the release of Visual Studio 2017. As mentioned on the .NET Blog by Mads Torgersen, C# 7 was focused on the consumption of data, simplifying code and improving performance. The biggest features to come out of C# 7 were *tuples* and *pattern matching*.

With tuples, developers can return more than one value from functions. Traditionally C# has allowed developers to return multiple values from a single function by building a structure and returning an instance of the structure.

You could also make use of out parameters which use the *out* keyword for each value being returned from the function. With C# 7, tuples provide an additional way of returning multiple values from a function.

The second big feature is *pattern matching* that can test if a value has a certain shape and then do something with that data. In this chapter we will be looking at these concepts and more. Here is what you can expect from this chapter:

- Getting started with tuples

- Pattern matching and deconstruction

- Using out variables

- Using local functions

- Generalized async return types

- Throw expressions

- Discards

C# 7 has so much to offer developers, it is definitely worth your while spending some time getting to know the new language features better. Grab a cup of coffee (if you don't have a cup already) and let's get started on our journey of discovering what C# 7 has to offer.

1

© Dirk Strauss 2019
D. Strauss, *Exploring Advanced Features in C#*, https://doi.org/10.1007/978-1-4842-4856-0_1

Please note that I have used Visual Studio Enterprise 2019 Preview for the code and screenshots in this book. You can download a copy from `https://visualstudio.microsoft.com`. Alternatively, you can continue using Visual Studio 2017, but be aware that you will not be able to run any of the code samples in the chapter on C# 8.0.

Getting Started with Tuples

Exactly what makes tuples so great? As you know, returning multiple values from a function is something you can already do in C#. Tuples simply give you another way to do this.

Create a class called `TupleExample`. Your Visual Studio project might look something as in Figure 1-1.

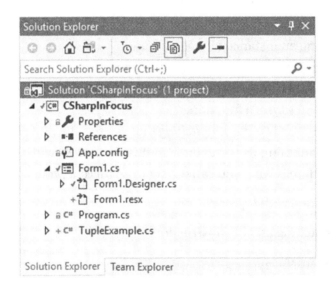

Figure 1-1. *Visual Studio Solution*

Next, add a tuple-returning function to the class called `GetGuitarType`. In its simplest form, a tuple-returning function looks as follows.

Listing 1-1. Tuple-returning function

```
public (string, int) GetGuitarType()
{
    return ("Les Paul Studio", 6);
}
```

All that this function does is return a tuple with a guitar type as a string and the number of strings it has as an integer to the calling code. Because this code is in a class, you would simply call it as follows.

Listing 1-2. Calling tuple-returning function

```
TupleExample te = new TupleExample();
var guitarResult = te.GetGuitarType();

Debug.WriteLine(guitarResult.Item1);
Debug.WriteLine(guitarResult.Item2);
```

Because I am using a Windows Forms project to demonstrate the use of tuples, I am simply writing out the result of the tuple to the output window in Visual Studio by using Debug.WriteLine. You can do this whichever way you like to.

If you look at the output window, you will notice that the values returned from the function are displayed.

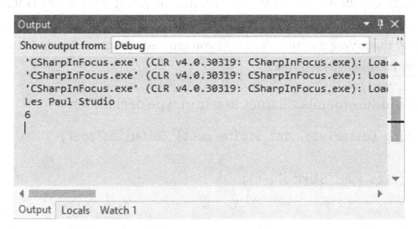

Figure 1-2. *Output from the returned tuple*

The easiest way to return tuples is to use an implicit variable which is declared using the var keyword. What is important to notice though is the use of the *Item1* and *Item2* in the guitarResult variable. You will see that by default the values returned in the tuple have been given positional names (Item1, Item2, Item3, etc.) depending on how many values you are returning.

You will notice that when you dot on the guitarResult variable, the Intellisense brings back the positional names of the tuple values.

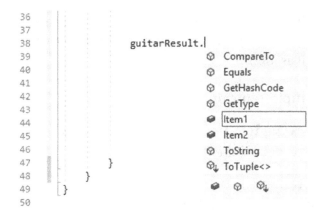

Figure 1-3. *Positional names of the tuple variable*

Changing the Default Positional Names for Tuple Values

You might be wondering if it is possible to change the default positional names for the tuple values. Luckily for us, the answer is a resounding yes. It is possible to include new default member names as part of the return type declaration for the tuple function.

Start off by modifying the tuple function you created earlier and include logical names for the members as follows.

Listing 1-3. Adding member names to return type declaration

```
public (string GuitarType, int StringCount) GetGuitarType()
{
    return ("Les Paul Studio", 6);
}
```

For the string return type, I specified that it should be identified by the member name GuitarType. For the integer return type, it will be identified as StringCount.

This time if you dot on the guitarResult variable, you will notice that the *Item1* and *Item2* positional names have been replaced by the member names we defined in the return type declaration.

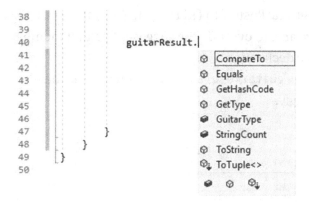

Figure 1-4. *Member names replace positional names*

You can still use *Item1*, *Item2*, and so on to refer to the tuple values. That still works, but now you can explicitly refer to the member names as follows.

Listing 1-4. Reference member names for tuple values

```
TupleExample te = new TupleExample();
var guitarResult = te.GetGuitarType();

Debug.WriteLine(guitarResult.GuitarType);
Debug.WriteLine(guitarResult.StringCount);
```

This makes it much easier to refer to values returned by the tuple function and clears up any confusion (and possible bugs) that would result by using the positional names.

Create Local Tuple Variables in the Return Data

You can probably guess that by referring to the tuple member names as default member names, you are able to define locally relevant names for them too. This is 100% correct. Let me clarify the previous statement.

The member names you specified for the tuple values are only suggested names. That is to say, the *GuitarType* and *StringCount* names are only suggested names. When you work with the return value, you are able to specify locally relevant member names. This means that if I do not want to call the members *GuitarType* and *StringCount*, then I can change that.

By changing `var guitarResult` to `(string BrandType, int GuitarStringCount)` `guitarResult`, you are able to override the suggested default member names declared in the tuple return type declaration.

When you dot on the `guitarResult` variable, you will see that the member names have changed accordingly.

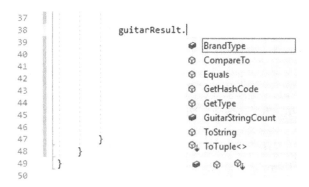

Figure 1-5. *Local member names for tuple values*

This means that our calling code will need to change to reference the locally relevant member names and will look as follows.

Listing 1-5. Local tuple variables

```
TupleExample te = new TupleExample();
(string BrandType, int GuitarStringCount) guitarResult = te.GetGuitarType();

Debug.WriteLine(guitarResult.BrandType);
Debug.WriteLine(guitarResult.GuitarStringCount);
```

You do not have to be tied into the default member names as defined in the return type declaration of the tuple function. Creating your own locally declared names gives you a lot more flexibility when working with tuples.

Tuple Members as Discrete Variables

C# 7 allows you to use tuple members as discrete variables. You will see that the code is quite similar to creating local tuple variables. The only difference here is the omission of the `guitarResult` variable. You will remember that our code used to assign the tuple returned from the function into the `guitarResult` variable by doing the following.

Listing 1-6. Returning local tuple variables

```
(string BrandType, int GuitarStringCount) guitarResult = te.GetGuitarType();
```

With discrete variables we can simply drop the guitarResult variable to produce the following code.

Listing 1-7. Discrete tuple variables

```
(string BrandType, int GuitarStringCount) = te.GetGuitarType();
```

Putting all the code together, you will see that one can now use BrandType and GuitarStringCount on their own.

Listing 1-8. Using the discrete tuple variables

```
TupleExample te = new TupleExample();
(string BrandType, int GuitarStringCount) = te.GetGuitarType();

Debug.WriteLine(BrandType);
Debug.WriteLine(GuitarStringCount);
```

In C# we refer to this as *deconstruction*. You don't need to explicitly declare the type of each field in the parentheses either. You can declare implicitly typed variables for each of the fields by using the var keyword.

Listing 1-9. Implicitly typed variables using var

```
TupleExample te = new TupleExample();
var (BrandType, GuitarStringCount) = te.GetGuitarType();

Debug.WriteLine(BrandType);
Debug.WriteLine(GuitarStringCount);
```

In Listing 1-9 the var keyword was outside the parentheses. You are also allowed to mix things up a bit by using the var keyword with any or all the variables that are declared inside the parentheses. Consider the following code example.

Listing 1-10. Using var with some of the variables

```
TupleExample te = new TupleExample();
(string BrandType, var GuitarStringCount) = te.GetGuitarType();

Debug.WriteLine(BrandType);
Debug.WriteLine(GuitarStringCount);
```

If you think that discrete variables are fancy, you should check out instances of tuple variables. Let's see how to do this next.

Instances of Tuple Variables

C# 7 allows you to use tuples as instance variables. This means that you can declare a variable as a tuple. To illustrate this, start off by creating a method called `PlayInstrument` that accepts a tuple as a parameter. All this will do is just output a line of text.

Listing 1-11. The PlayInstrument method

```
private void PlayInstrument((string, int) instrumentToPlay)
{
    Debug.WriteLine($"I am playing a {instrumentToPlay.Item1} with
    {instrumentToPlay.Item2} strings");
}
```

You will need to create an `enum` called `InstrumentType` that has several instruments. The enum is simply `public enum InstrumentType { guitar, cello, violin }` and is used at the top of your class file. You can then use the enum in the following code along with the instances of tuple variables.

Listing 1-12. Using tuples as instance variables

```
string instrumentType = nameof(InstrumentType.guitar);
int strings = 12;
(string TypeOfInstrument, int NumberOfStrings) instrument = (instrumentType,
strings);
PlayInstrument(instrument);
```

You will notice that I pass an instance of the tuple variable called `instrument` to the `PlayInstrument` method. Inside the `PlayInstrument` method, I refer to the tuple values by using the positional names of the tuple values. I could also have written the `PlayInstrument` method as follows.

Listing 1-13. PlayInstrument method using custom member names

```
private void PlayInstrument((string instrument, int strings) instrumentToPlay)
{
    Debug.WriteLine($"I am playing a {instrumentToPlay.instrument} with
    {instrumentToPlay.strings} strings");
}
```

This is a more natural way of referencing the tuple values.

Comparing Tuples

You can also compare tuple members. To illustrate this, let's stay with the musical instruments and compare the string counts of a guitar and a violin.

Start off by using the enum you created earlier and create the following tuple type variables.

Listing 1-14. Creating tuple type variables

```
string instrumentType1 = nameof(InstrumentType.guitar);
int stringsCount1 = 6;
(string TypeOfInstrument, int NumberOfStrings) instrument1 = (instrumentType1,
stringsCount1);

string instrumentType2 = nameof(InstrumentType.violin);
int stringsCount2 = 4;
(string TypeOfInstrument, int NumberOfStrings) instrument2 = (instrumentType2,
stringsCount2);
```

A violin and a guitar have different string counts. The guitar has six while the violin only has four. Checking the equality of the count is as easy as using an `if` statement.

Listing 1-15. Comparing tuple members

```
if (instrument1.NumberOfStrings != instrument2.NumberOfStrings)
{
    Debug.WriteLine($"A {instrument2.TypeOfInstrument} does not have the
    same number of strings as a {instrument1.TypeOfInstrument}");
}
```

You can also compare the entire tuple variables with each other. Prior to version 7.3, checking tuple equality used to require the Equals method.

Listing 1-16. Comparing tuples before C# 7.3

```
if (!instrument1.Equals(instrument2))
{
    Debug.WriteLine("We are dealing with different instruments here.");
}
```

If you tried using == or != with tuple types, you would see an error.

```
if (instrument1 == instrument2)

        [@] (local variable) (string TypeOfInstrument, int NumberOfStrings) instrument1

}       Feature 'tuple equality' is not available in C# 7.0. Please use language version 7.3 or greater.

        Show potential fixes (Alt+Enter or Ctrl+.)
```

Figure 1-6. *Tuple equality error in C# 7.0*

To test tuple equality by using == or != you need to have C# 7.3 or greater. To use this version of C#, you need to do the following:

1. Right-click the project and click *Properties*.

2. On the *Build* tab, click the *Advanced* button.

3. On the Advanced Build Settings, set the Language version to the latest minor version.

This is enough to select C# 7.3 (in our case) to use in the project.

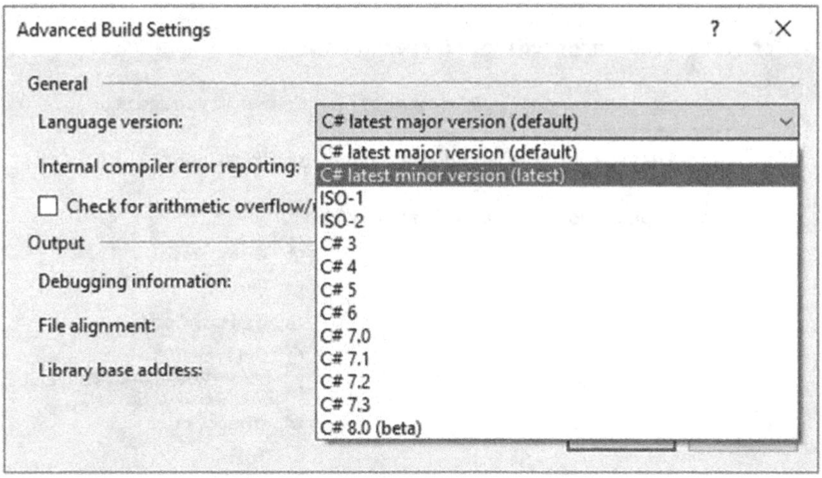

Figure 1-7. *Selecting the C# language version*

Take note that C# 8.0 (beta) is available in this list. This is because I am using Visual Studio 2019 Preview. If you are using Visual Studio 2017, you will not see C# 8.0.

After you have selected your C# language version, swing back to your code and look at the line we saw the error on earlier. The error has gone away. Personally I am not too fond of using ! on the Equals method. It obscures the readability for me somewhat.

The line if (instrument1 != instrument2) reads more natural to me than if (!instrument1.Equals(instrument2)).

Inferring Tuple Element Names

Starting with C# 7.1, a small enhancement was made to the C# language to infer tuple element names. Consider the following block of code.

Listing 1-17. Inferring tuple element names

```
string instrumentType = nameof(InstrumentType.guitar);
int stringsCount = 6;
var instrument = (instrumentType, stringsCount);
```

When I dot on the instrument variable, the IntelliSense shows me the member names inferred from the variables used to initialize the tuple.

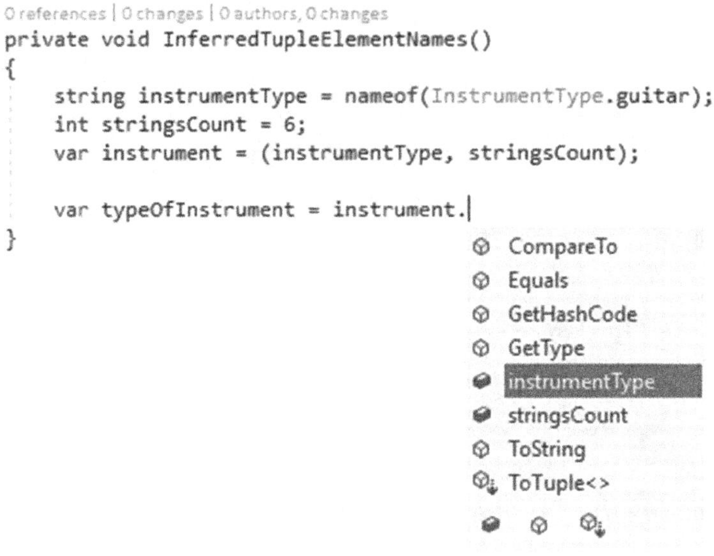

```
0 references | 0 changes | 0 authors, 0 changes
private void InferredTupleElementNames()
{
    string instrumentType = nameof(InstrumentType.guitar);
    int stringsCount = 6;
    var instrument = (instrumentType, stringsCount);

    var typeOfInstrument = instrument.|
}
```

⊘ CompareTo
⊘ Equals
⊘ GetHashCode
⊘ GetType
● instrumentType
● stringsCount
⊘ ToString
⊘₊ ToTuple<>

●   ⊘   ⊘₊

Figure 1-8. *Inferred member names*

This is a welcome enhancement to C# 7, starting with version 7.1.

The Ways to Deconstruct Tuples

The term *tuple deconstruction* simply means to take all the items in a tuple and splitting them out in a single operation. In fact, the code listings in this section have already been doing that.

You will hear the term frequently, as this refers to something that is done naturally when working with tuples. The following figure illustrates the ways in which tuple deconstruction can take place.

```
1 reference | 0 changes | 0 authors, 0 changes
private void DeconstructingTuplesExplicit()
{
    // Explicitly declare each field's type
    TupleExample te = new TupleExample();
    (string BrandType, int GuitarStringCount) = te.GetGuitarType();
}
1 reference | 0 changes | 0 authors, 0 changes
private void DeconstructingTuplesInferring()
{
    // Inferring the type of each variable with the var keyword
    TupleExample te = new TupleExample();
    var (BrandType, GuitarStringCount) = te.GetGuitarType();
}
2 references | 0 changes | 0 authors, 0 changes
private void DeconstructingTuplesIndividualInference()
{
    // Inferring the type of each variable individually with the var keyword
    TupleExample te = new TupleExample();
    (string BrandType, var GuitarStringCount) = te.GetGuitarType();
}
1 reference | 0 changes | 0 authors, 0 changes
private void DeconstructingTuplesPrevVariables()
{
    // Deconstruct into previously declared variables
    TupleExample te = new TupleExample();
    string BrandType = "";
    int GuitarStringCount = 6;
    (BrandType, GuitarStringCount) = te.GetGuitarType();
}
```

Figure 1-9. *Deconstructing tuples*

As you can see, there are essentially only four ways to perform tuple deconstruction.

There are actually only three ways, but I counted the two ways to use inference as a separate deconstruction method.

These methods for deconstruction are

- Explicitly declaring each field's type

- Inferring the type of each variable with a single var keyword

- Inferring the type of the variables by mixing the var keyword with any or all variable declarations

- Declaring variables and deconstructing the tuple into the previously declared variables

For me, using a single `var` keyword is probably the most efficient way of deconstructing a tuple. The other methods are a bit long-winded for my liking. I guess it all comes down to personal preference really.

Whichever method you use to deconstruct a tuple, the fact that I can do that in a single deconstruct operation is a welcome feature indeed.

Final Thoughts on Tuples

Tuples definitely have a place in your everyday coding practice. Using them often will help in understanding them better. Note that tuples can have more than just the two members I have been using in the code examples. It would probably not be a good idea to create a tuple with so many members that it becomes unwieldy to manage and work with.

In C#, `Tuple.Create` allows a maximum of eight items. In practice this is usually sufficient. But if you find yourself creating tuples with a lot of members, then perhaps you need to consider using a class or a structure. It is incredible what some musicians can achieve on a couple of stringed instruments. It is even more incredible what developers can achieve with tuples.

Pattern Matching

In C# 7, we now have the ability to use pattern matching. By using patterns, we can test if a value has a certain *shape* and, if so, work with the information of that matching shape.

In fact, you are already using pattern matching algorithms when you use the `if` and `switch` statements to test values. If the statements match, you take the matched value and extract its information.

In C# 7 you can use new syntax elements which extend the `is` and `switch` statements which you are already familiar with. Let's start off with creating a new class called `PatternMatchingExample` and adding our code to this class.

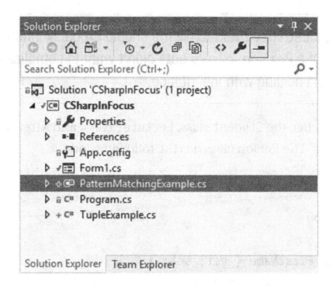

Figure 1-10. *PatternMatchingExample class*

I have created the following enums on the PatternMatchingExample class.

Listing 1-18. Class enums

```
public enum UniversityCourses { Maths, Chemistry, Anatomy, LifeSkills }
public enum UniversityDegree { BA, BSc }
```

I am not going into detail for each class used in this example. You can download the source code for this book and work with the examples as you need to.

For now, assume that we have the following objects:

- Person class

- Student class (which inherits from Person class)

- Lecturer class (which inherits from Person class)

- Alumnus class (which inherits from Person class)

- ExchangeStudent struct

The classes are all similar with slight differences which I'll briefly highlight here. We also have a struct for ExchangeStudent.

> Strictly speaking, a Lecturer and Alumnus should probably inherit from a Student instead of a Person class but I didn't want to complicate things. After all, this chapter isn't dealing with inheritance.

As mentioned earlier, the Student class, Lecturer class, and Alumnus class all inherit from the Person class. The Person class has the following code.

Listing 1-19. Person class code

```
public class Person
{
    public string FirstName { get; set; }
    public string LastName { get; set; }
    public int Age { get; set; }
}
```

The Student class has a property for the course that the student is enrolled in. It also returns unique values from the StudentDetails method. The Student class has the following definition.

Listing 1-20. Student class code

```
public class Student : Person
{
    public int StudentNumber { get; }
    public UniversityCourses CourseEnrolledFor { get; }
    public Student((string firstname, string lastname, int age)
    personDetails, int studentNumber, UniversityCourses courseEnrolled)
    {
        FirstName = personDetails.firstname;
        LastName = personDetails.lastname;
        Age = personDetails.age;
        StudentNumber = studentNumber;
        CourseEnrolledFor = courseEnrolled;
    }
```

```
    public (string fullName, int studentNum, string studentCourse)
    StudentDetails()
    {
        var studentDetails = ($"{FirstName} {LastName}", StudentNumber,
        CourseEnrolledFor.ToString());
        return studentDetails;
    }
}
```

The other classes return different properties from the method that returns that particular object's details. The Lecturer class, for example, contains a property for the course specialization that the lecturer teaches. Its details method however calculates and returns the number of days that the lecturer has been employed. This is the code for the Lecturer class.

Listing 1-21. Lecturer class code

```
public class Lecturer : Person
{
    public int EmployeeNumber { get; }
    public string CourseSpecialization { get; }
    public DateTime DateEmployed { get; }
    public Lecturer((string firstname, string lastname, int
    age) personDetails, int employeeNumber, UniversityCourses
    courseSpecialization, DateTime dateEmployed)
    {
        FirstName = personDetails.firstname;
        LastName = personDetails.lastname;
        Age = personDetails.age;
        EmployeeNumber = employeeNumber;
        CourseSpecialization = courseSpecialization.ToString();
        DateEmployed = dateEmployed;
    }

    public (string fullName, int employeeNum, string courseSpecial, int
    totalDayesEmployed) LecturerDetails()
    {
```

```
        double lengthOfServiceInDays = DateTime.Now.Subtract(DateEmployed).
        TotalDays;
        var lecturerDetails = ($"{FirstName} {LastName}", EmployeeNumber,
        CourseSpecialization, Convert.ToInt32(lengthOfServiceInDays));
        return lecturerDetails;
    }
}
```

The Alumnus has completed their degree, so the Alumnus class contains a property for the degree that they obtained and the year they completed their degree. The Alumnus class looks as follows.

Listing 1-22. Alumnus class code

```
public class Alumnus : Person
{
    public int YearCompleted { get; }
    public UniversityDegree DegreeObtained { get; }
    public Alumnus((string firstname, string lastname, int age)
    personDetails, int yearStudiesCompleted, UniversityDegree degreeObtained)
    {
        FirstName = personDetails.firstname;
        LastName = personDetails.lastname;
        Age = personDetails.age;
        YearCompleted = yearStudiesCompleted;
        DegreeObtained = degreeObtained;
    }

    public (string fullName, int yearCompleted, string degreeObtained)
    AlumnusDetails()
    {
        var alumnusDetails = ($"{FirstName} {LastName}", YearCompleted,
        DegreeObtained.ToString());
        return alumnusDetails;
    }
}
```

Lastly, the ExchangeStudent is a struct and contains a property for the short course they attended and the number of days left on their student visa. The ExchangeStudent struct looks as follows.

Listing 1-23. ExchangeStudent struct code

```
public struct ExchangeStudent
{
    public string FirstName { get; }
    public string LastName { get; }
    public string ShortCourse { get; }
    public DateTime VisaExpiryDate { get; }

    public ExchangeStudent((string firstname, string lastname, int
    age) personDetails, UniversityCourses shortCourse, DateTime
    studentVisaExpiryDate)
    {
        FirstName = personDetails.firstname;
        LastName = personDetails.lastname;
        ShortCourse = shortCourse.ToString();
        VisaExpiryDate = studentVisaExpiryDate;
    }

    public (string fullName, string shortCourse, int daysLeftOnVisa)
    ExchangeStudentDetails()
    {
        double lenOfVisa = VisaExpiryDate.Subtract(DateTime.Now).TotalDays;

        var exchangeDetails = ($"{FirstName} {LastName}", ShortCourse,
        Convert.ToInt32(lenOfVisa));
        return exchangeDetails;
    }
}
```

If we have a specific object, we want to get the correct details for that object. You will notice that we are returning the information from each class in a tuple.

The design of our classes isn't important here. What is important is the way we determine its shape and then, based on that, extract the data to work with. We will now see how pattern matching works on each of these objects.

Using the Is Type Pattern Expression

Before C# 7 you would have had to test the type of the object using a series of if and is statements. This is a classic type pattern and you are testing a variable to figure out what type it is.

Based on the type of the variable, you perform a different action. An example of such code would probably look like the following.

Listing 1-24. Pre-C# 7 type testing

```
// Before C# 7
if (someperson is Student)
{
    var student = (Student)someperson;
    return $"{student.StudentDetails().fullName} is enrolled for {student.
    StudentDetails().studentCourse} with student number {student.
    StudentDetails().studentNum}";
}
else if (someperson is Lecturer)
{
    var lecturer = (Lecturer)someperson;
    return $"{lecturer.LecturerDetails().fullName} teaches {lecturer.
    LecturerDetails().courseSpecial}";
}
else if (someperson is Alumnus)
{
    var alumnus = (Alumnus)someperson;
    return $"{alumnus.AlumnusDetails().fullName} has completed {alumnus.
    AlumnusDetails().degreeObtained} in {alumnus.AlumnusDetails().
    yearCompleted}";
}
```

Fast forward to C# 7 and we have a simpler, more concise way of doing this. In the following code, we are using the extended is expression that assigns a variable if the test succeeds. The code looks as follows.

Listing 1-25. The is type pattern expression

```
// The is type pattern
if (someperson is Student student)
{
    return $"{student.StudentDetails().fullName} is enrolled for {student.
    StudentDetails().studentCourse} with student number {student.
    StudentDetails().studentNum}";
}
else if (someperson is Lecturer lecturer)
{
    return $"{lecturer.LecturerDetails().fullName} teaches {lecturer.
    LecturerDetails().courseSpecial}";
}
else if (someperson is Alumnus alumnus)
{
    return $"{alumnus.AlumnusDetails().fullName} has completed {alumnus.
    AlumnusDetails().degreeObtained} in {alumnus.AlumnusDetails().
    yearCompleted}";
}
else if (someperson is ExchangeStudent exchStudent)
{
    return $"{exchStudent.ExchangeStudentDetails().fullName} has
    {exchStudent.ExchangeStudentDetails().daysLeftOnVisa} days left on
    Student Visa";
}
```

We now have a shortcut by using the is expression. This is because it does two things. It tests the variable and it assigns it to a new variable. Also notice that I have included the ExchangeStudent type which is a struct. This means that the new is expression will happily work with value types (structs) and reference types (classes).

A side note on structs and classes: When creating a struct, the variable assigned to the struct holds the struct's actual data. When it is assigned to a new variable, it is copied which gives the new variable a separate space in memory. The original variable and the new variable now contain two separate copies of the same data. This is what we call a value type.

A class is a reference type. A reference type contains a pointer to another memory location that holds the data.

The extended is expression makes for somewhat shorter code and is more readable. Another point to take note of is the newly created variable after each is expression. These are only in scope and assigned when the pattern matching expressions return true results.

Using Switch Pattern Matching Statements

In the previous section, we had a look at the is pattern matching expression. It required if statements on each type you needed to check. This can become somewhat cumbersome as it also only tests if the input matches a single type. This is where the switch expression can come in handy.

Traditional switch statements only supported the constant pattern. It also only supported numeric types and the string type. In C# 7 you can now use the type pattern. This means that we can do the following.

Listing 1-26. Switch pattern matching statements

```
// Using switch statements pattern matching
switch (someperson)
{
    case Student student:
        return $"{student.StudentDetails().fullName} is enrolled for
        {student.StudentDetails().studentCourse} with student number
        {student.StudentDetails().studentNum}";
    case Lecturer lecturer:
        return $"{lecturer.LecturerDetails().fullName} teaches {lecturer.
        LecturerDetails().courseSpecial}";
```

```
    case Alumnus alumnus:
        return $"{alumnus.AlumnusDetails().fullName} has completed
        {alumnus.AlumnusDetails().degreeObtained} in {alumnus.
        AlumnusDetails().yearCompleted}";
    case ExchangeStudent exchangeStudent:
        return $"{exchangeStudent.ExchangeStudentDetails().fullName} has
        {exchangeStudent.ExchangeStudentDetails().daysLeftOnVisa} days left
        on Student Visa";
}
```

Whenever a case statement is evaluated to true, the code beneath it is run. In C# 7 the restrictions on variable types have been removed from `switch` expressions, and any type may be used.

Using When Clauses in Case Expressions

We can cater for special conditions by using a when clause on the case label. Let us assume that we also want to identify senior alumni. These individuals will have completed their course before 1976.

We can therefore use a when clause on the case label to check for this condition. Consider then the following code listing.

Listing 1-27. Using a when clause

```
// Using switch statements pattern matching
switch (someperson)
{
    case Student student:
        return $"{student.StudentDetails().fullName} is enrolled for
        {student.StudentDetails().studentCourse} with student number
        {student.StudentDetails().studentNum}";
    case Lecturer lecturer:
        return $"{lecturer.LecturerDetails().fullName} teaches {lecturer.
        LecturerDetails().courseSpecial}";
    case Alumnus alumnus when alumnus.YearCompleted <= 1975: // Note the
    when keyword here
        return $"{alumnus.AlumnusDetails().fullName} is a senior Alumnus";
```

```
    case Alumnus alumnus:
        return $"{alumnus.AlumnusDetails().fullName} has completed
        {alumnus.AlumnusDetails().degreeObtained} in {alumnus.
        AlumnusDetails().yearCompleted}";
    case ExchangeStudent exchangeStudent:
        return $"{exchangeStudent.ExchangeStudentDetails().fullName} has
        {exchangeStudent.ExchangeStudentDetails().daysLeftOnVisa} days left
        on Student Visa";
}
```

If the YearCompleted value is <= 1975, we return a slightly different message to the calling code.

If the code is slightly difficult to understand, consider downloading the source code for the book and following along in Visual Studio.

Another interesting thing to note is that multiple case labels can be grouped together under a single switch section. Consider the following code.

Listing 1-28. Multiple case labels

```
// Using multiple case labels in switch statements
switch (someperson)
{
    case Student student when student.CourseEnrolledFor == UniversityCourses.
    Chemistry:
    case Alumnus alumnus when alumnus.DegreeObtained == UniversityDegree.BSc:
        return "Chemistry and BSc excluded";
    case Student student:
        return $"{student.StudentDetails().fullName} is enrolled for
        {student.StudentDetails().studentCourse} with student number
        {student.StudentDetails().studentNum}";
    case Lecturer lecturer:
        return $"{lecturer.LecturerDetails().fullName} teaches {lecturer.
        LecturerDetails().courseSpecial}";
```

```
        case Alumnus alumnus when alumnus.YearCompleted <= 1975:
            return $"{alumnus.AlumnusDetails().fullName} is a senior Alumnus";
        case Alumnus alumnus:
            return $"{alumnus.AlumnusDetails().fullName} has completed {alumnus.
            AlumnusDetails().degreeObtained} in {alumnus.AlumnusDetails().
            yearCompleted}";
        case ExchangeStudent exchangeStudent:
            return $"{exchangeStudent.ExchangeStudentDetails().fullName} has
            {exchangeStudent.ExchangeStudentDetails().daysLeftOnVisa} days left
            on Student Visa";
}
```

Here you see that we want to exclude the chemistry students and the BSc alumni. The example of excluding those object types based on course enrolled for or degree obtained is rather silly (i.e., probably not a great real-world example). It does however highlight an important feature of the switch statements:

- I can apply multiple case labels to a single switch section.

- The order of each section matters.

So, what do I mean when I say that the order of the sections matter? Well consider the effects of adding the code case Student student as the first case in the switch statement. This will cause the case with the when clause for student never to be evaluated.

In fact, the code in Listing 1-28 is already going to exclude senior alumni because the first case label that excludes alumni based on the degree obtained will include any senior alumni. Therefore, a senior alumnus that obtained a BSc degree will always be excluded from the senior alumnus evaluation further down the switch statement. To demonstrate this, consider the following objects.

Listing 1-29. Alumnus objects

```
Alumnus alumnus = new Alumnus(("Gabby", "Salinger", 26), 2017,
UniversityDegree.BSc);
Alumnus senalumnus = new Alumnus(("Frank", "Greer", 74), 1970,
UniversityDegree.BSc);
```

Running the code and passing it two instances of the Alumnus class will result in the output of Chemistry and BSc excluded for both objects. To overcome this issue, we can add in the conditional logical AND operator.

The && operator is also known as a short-circuiting logical AND operator. It computes the logical AND of the bool operands which evaluates to true if both sides of the && evaluate to true. Therefore, if the first condition is false, the expression short-circuits out immediately. This means that the second condition will only be evaluated if the first condition is true.

To illustrate this and to allow the senior alumni to still be evaluated, modify your switch statement as follows.

Listing 1-30. Modified switch statement to cater for senior alumni

```
// Modified switch statement to cater for senior alumni
switch (someperson)
{
    case Student student when student.CourseEnrolledFor ==
    UniversityCourses.Chemistry:
    case Alumnus alumnus when alumnus.DegreeObtained == UniversityDegree.
    BSc && alumnus.YearCompleted > 1975:
        return "Chemistry and BSc excluded";
    case Student student:
        return $"{student.StudentDetails().fullName} is enrolled for
        {student.StudentDetails().studentCourse} with student number
        {student.StudentDetails().studentNum}";
    case Lecturer lecturer:
        return $"{lecturer.LecturerDetails().fullName} teaches {lecturer.
        LecturerDetails().courseSpecial}";
    case Alumnus alumnus when alumnus.YearCompleted <= 1975:
        return $"{alumnus.AlumnusDetails().fullName} is a senior Alumnus";
    case Alumnus alumnus:
        return $"{alumnus.AlumnusDetails().fullName} has completed
        {alumnus.AlumnusDetails().degreeObtained} in {alumnus.
        AlumnusDetails().yearCompleted}";
```

```
    case ExchangeStudent exchangeStudent:
        return $"{exchangeStudent.ExchangeStudentDetails().fullName} has
        {exchangeStudent.ExchangeStudentDetails().daysLeftOnVisa} days left
        on Student Visa";
}
```

All that we have done is add `&& alumnus.YearCompleted > 1975` to the when clause of the alumnus `case` label. Essentially, I am saying that the `Alumnus` object must only be excluded when the alumnus obtained a BSc degree and the year that the degree was obtained is after 1975.

If I used the same `Alumnus` objects in Listing 1-29 and ran my code, I would see different results in the output window.

Listing 1-31. Output window results

```
Chemistry and BSc excluded
Frank Greer is a senior Alumnus
```

While the first `Alumnus` object is excluded based on the degree obtained, the second is passed through the `case` because the condition of having the degree obtained after 1975 was not met. Senior alumni are therefore still evaluated.

As you will see, the order of each section definitely matters. A general rule of thumb is to keep the most restrictive `case` labels at the top of the `switch` statement while having the most general `case` label at the end.

Checking for Nulls in Switch Statements

We are able to check for `null` by adding a `null` case. This ensures that the argument passed to the switch statement is not null. Consider the following code.

Listing 1-32. Null case

```
// Cater for null
switch (someperson)
{
    case Student student:
        return $"{student.StudentDetails().fullName}";
```

```
        case Lecturer lecturer:
            return $"{lecturer.LecturerDetails().fullName}";
        case Alumnus alumnus:
            return $"{alumnus.AlumnusDetails().fullName}";
        case ExchangeStudent exchangeStudent:
            return $"{exchangeStudent.ExchangeStudentDetails().fullName}";
        case null:
            return $"{nameof(someperson)} cannot be null";
}
```

Passing a null object to this switch statement will result in the null case being evaluated and the message *someperson cannot be null* returned.

Pattern matching is a fantastic way to control the flow of your code logic. Some consider it to be syntactic sugar. Whatever your thoughts are on pattern matching, it's definitely great to be able to use it in C# 7.

Using Out Variables

The out keyword in C# has been around for a while. Using out passes arguments by reference. By default, all parameters in C# are passed by value unless you explicitly include an out or ref modifier. In the past, you would have to declare a variable to use as an out parameter.

This has changed in C# 7 and you are able to declare the variable right there where you use it. Imagine that we wanted to test if a variable is a valid integer value. This is how our code used to look before C# 7.

Listing 1-33. Pre-C#7 code for out keyword

```
string num = "123";
int numParsed;
if (int.TryParse(num, out numParsed))
{
    Debug.WriteLine($"{num} is a valid integer");
}
```

```
else
{
    Debug.WriteLine($"{num} is not a valid integer");
}
```

We have this integer variable called numParsed that just sort of hangs around. In C# 7 we can now do the following.

Listing 1-34. C# 7 code for out keyword

```
string num = "123";
if (int.TryParse(num, out int numParsed))
{
    Debug.WriteLine($"{num} is a valid integer");
}
else
{
    Debug.WriteLine($"{num} is not a valid integer");
}
```

Do you see the difference? Blink and you might miss it. We no longer have to declare a funny loose standing variable that hangs around before our TryParse check.

It's a small but welcome change to the C# language. Another point to note is that the compiler is able to infer the type of the numParsed variable which means we can use the var keyword too.

This just means that instead of using out int, we can use out var and achieve the same results. Consider the following code listing.

Listing 1-35. Using var with out

```
string num = "123";
if (int.TryParse(num, out var numParsed))
{
    Debug.WriteLine($"{num} is a valid integer");
}
else
{
    Debug.WriteLine($"{num} is not a valid integer");
}
```

Then there is another small addition in C# 7 that might have slipped past a few developers out there. That is the inclusion of *discards*. It makes sense to discuss discards now, seeing as it is supported in the context of out parameters.

Discards

In C# 7, the language now supports discards. Think of these as dummy variables that are temporary and will not be used in your application code. In other words, you don't actually care about the value assigned. Using discards is the same as using unassigned variables because the variable itself does not contain a value.

This means that the discard variable may not even be allocated a storage space which in turn reduces memory allocations. Discard variables are supported in the following contexts within C# 7:

- Tuples and object deconstruction
- Pattern matching with is and switch
- The out parameters used in method calls
- Standalone discard variable when no other discard variable is in scope

To indicate that a variable is a discard, you need to assign it the underscore character as its variable name. Taking the previous listing for the out parameter, we can make a small change and use a discard variable. Consider the following code listing.

Listing 1-36. Using discards with out parameters

```
string num = "123";
if (int.TryParse(num, out _))
{
    Debug.WriteLine($"{num} is a valid integer");
}
else
{
    Debug.WriteLine($"{num} is not a valid integer");
}
```

The only portion that I have changed is that I have replaced `int.TryParse(num, out var numParsed)` with `int.TryParse(num, out _)`. This is really nice and totally negates the need for that unnecessary `numParsed` variable declaration.

I will be discussing discards later on in this chapter, so stick around. Next, we will be having a look at what local functions are and how to use them in C# 7.

Using Local Functions

Local functions are private methods that are nested in another method. The use of local functions is quite common in functional languages. This has now been included in C# 7.

The use of local functions is really limited to the containing method. This means that only the containing method can call the local function. The use of local functions should therefore make sense within the confines of the containing member and should actually only have value within the containing member.

For this reason, using local functions makes the intent of your code clearer to someone reading it. This is because you will know that the local function is *only* callable by the containing member and nowhere else. Local functions can be declared and called from the following members:

- Methods, anonymous methods, and constructors
- Property accessors and event accessors
- Lambda expressions
- Finalizers
- Other local functions

Let's have a look at an example of a local function. In this example I will be creating classes for different objects. The local function will be added to my class constructor and will calculate the volume of the shape. The constructor will be responsible for determining the object description.

Start off by adding a class called LocalFunctionExample to your project. Then create a constructor for this class. It is here that we will be adding all our code.

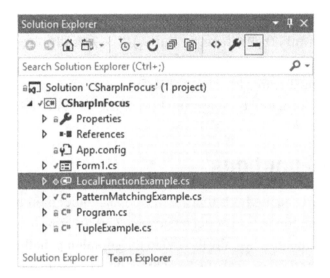

Figure 1-11. *LocalFunctionExample class*

Go ahead and create classes for objects you can calculate the volume for. I used the following objects:

- Cube

- Pyramid

- Sphere

Each object differs obviously in shape; therefore, each class caters for the dimensions needed to determine the volume of each object. Here is the code for the Cube class, Pyramid class, and Sphere class.

Listing 1-37. The object classes' code

```
public class Cube
{
    public double Edge { get; }
    public Cube(double edgeLength)
    {
        Edge = edgeLength;
    }
}
```

```
public class Pyramid
{
    public double BaseLength { get; }
    public double BaseWidth { get; }
    public double Height { get; }
    public Pyramid(double triangleBaseLength, double triangleBaseWidth,
    double triangleHeight)
    {
        BaseLength = triangleBaseLength;
        BaseWidth = triangleBaseWidth;
        Height = triangleHeight;
    }
}

public class Sphere
{
    public double Radius { get; }
    public Sphere(double circleRadius)
    {
        Radius = circleRadius;
    }
}
```

Next, you need to create a constructor for your LocalFunctionExample class that will contain the logic needed to determine the object description and the local function to calculate the volume.

Pro tip To create constructors quickly, type *ctor* and hit the Tab key twice. Visual Studio will automatically insert the constructor for you.

Consider the following code for the LocalFunctionExample constructor.

Listing 1-38. The LocalFunctionExample class

```
public class LocalFunctionExample
{
    public double ObjectVolume { get; }
    public string ObjectType { get; }

    public LocalFunctionExample(object shapeObject)
    {

        double GetObjectVolume(object shape)
        {
            switch (shape)
            {
                case Cube square:
                    return Math.Pow(square.Edge, 3.00);
                case Pyramid triangle:
                    return (triangle.BaseLength * triangle.BaseWidth *
                    triangle.Height) / 3;
                case Sphere sphere:
                    return 4 * Math.PI * Math.Pow(sphere.Radius, 3) / 3;
                case null:
                    return 0.0;
            }

            return 0.0;
        }

        ObjectVolume = GetObjectVolume(shapeObject);
        ObjectType = ObjectVolume == 0.0 ? "Invalid Object Shape" :
        shapeObject.GetType().Name;
    }
}
```

What you will notice is that I have added a local function called GetObjectVolume that takes the object passed to the constructor and uses *pattern matching* to determine what type of object we are working with.

If any unrecognized shape is passed to the local function, the local function
will return a volume of 0.0 and this will result in the ternary conditional expression
displaying *Invalid Object Shape* as the ObjectType value.

To test the local function, add the following code and pass the objects to your
LocalFunctionExample class. Just use Debug.WriteLine to display the output from the
LocalFunctionExample class.

Listing 1-39. Testing the local function

```
Cube cube = new Cube(5);
Pyramid pyramid = new Pyramid(5, 5, 5);
Sphere sphere = new Sphere(5);
Student student = new Student(("john", "doe", 22), 12345,
UniversityCourses.Anatomy);
```

This will result in the following lines displayed in the output window.

Listing 1-40. Output

```
This is a Cube with a volume of 125
This is a Pyramid with a volume of 41,6666666666667
This is a Sphere with a volume of 523,598775598299
This is a Invalid Object Shape with a volume of 0
```

You can see that when we passed an unrecognized object to our constructor, the class
handled it with dropping through the switch statement and setting the volume to 0.0.

Here are a few more notes on local functions:

- All the local variables defined in the containing member can be
  accessed from the local function.

- All the method parameters can be accessed from the local function.

- Local functions are private; therefore they can't include access
  modifiers.

- You can't include the static keyword for local functions.

- You can't apply attributes to local functions or its parameters.

CHAPTER 1   C# 7 IN FOCUS

Local functions are quite nice when you want to use some functionality throughout a method, where that functionality only applies to its containing member. You will also notice that the local function was at the top of our constructor and the code that referred to it (that calculated the volume) came after the local function.

The position of this doesn't matter. You can just as easily call `ObjectVolume = GetObjectVolume(shapeObject);` before the local function code and still achieve the same output.

Generalized Async Return Types

The functionality of async/await is widely used to avoid performance bottlenecks and improve the responsiveness of your application. There is a slight issue though that in certain situations, returning a `Task` object from async methods could introduce performance issues.

This is especially evident when an `async` method returns a cached result or completes in a synchronous fashion. We know that the supported return types are `Task<T>`, `Task`, and `void`. In C# 7, the `ValueTask` type has been added to allow `async` methods to return other types in addition to the types I mentioned a minute ago.

This feature is best illustrated with an example. I will simply use a console application to illustrate the use of the `ValueTask` type. Before we can jump into writing code, we need to install the NuGet package `System.Threading.Tasks.Extensions` so that we can use the `ValueTask<TResult>` type.

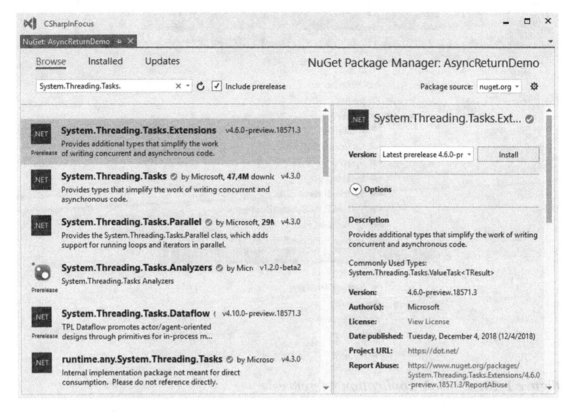

Figure 1-12. *NuGet Package Manager*

Once you have installed the NuGet package, you will see that System.Threading. Tasks.Extensions is listed in your project references.

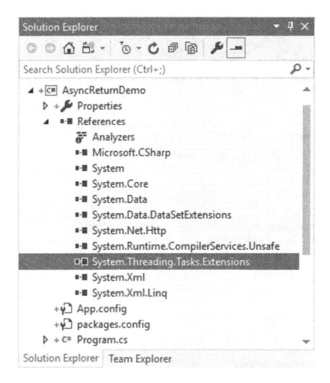

Figure 1-13. *Console application references*

Now we can start writing some code. The console application is a dummy share price ticker for the NASDAQ. For the share prices, I will obviously be using dummy data, but this should illustrate the performance gains of using the ValueTask type.

The application will loop 100 million times, but only read new stock information if the cache period has been exceeded. Start off by creating a StockListing class that will hold the stock information.

Listing 1-41. The StockListing class

```
public class StockListing
{
    public string NASDAQTickerSymbol { get; }
    public decimal Open { get; }
    public decimal High { get; }
    public decimal Low { get; }
    public string MarketCap { get; }
    public StockListing(string nasdaq, decimal open, decimal high, decimal
    low, string marketCap)
```

```
    {
        NASDAQTickerSymbol = nasdaq;
        Open = open;
        High = high;
        Low = low;
        MarketCap = marketCap;
    }
}
```

The next class will simply use the Task<T> to return the result of the stock lookup. The class includes a local function called GetShareDetails that reads the latest share information.

If, however, the cache time has not expired, then the cached stock listings are returned. The class code looks as follows.

Listing 1-42. ShareService class

```
public class ShareService
{
    private readonly TimeSpan cacheTime = TimeSpan.FromSeconds(2);
    private DateTime lastRun = DateTime.Now;
    private IEnumerable<StockListing> cachedListings;

    public async Task<IEnumerable<StockListing>> GetStockDetails()
    {
        async Task<IEnumerable<StockListing>> GetShareDetails()
        {
            cachedListings = await Task.Run(() => new List<StockListing>
            {
                new StockListing("AAPL", 157.50m, 158.52m, 154.55m,
                "741,37B")
                ,new StockListing("AMZN", 1473.35m, 1513.47m, 1449.00m,
                "722,71B")
                ,new StockListing("QCOM", 56.33m, 57.53m, 56.24m, "68,86B")
            });

            lastRun = DateTime.Now;
            WriteLine($"Get share details - {lastRun}");
```

```
        return cachedListings;
    }

    if (DateTime.Now - lastRun < cacheTime)
    {
        return cachedListings;
    }

    return await GetShareDetails();
    }
}
```

From the console application, we use the service in the following manner.

Listing 1-43. Calling the service from the console application

```
static void Main(string[] args)
{
    var shareListing = new ShareService();
    for (int i = 0; i < 100_000_000; i++)
    {
        var result = shareListing.GetStockDetails().Result;
    }

    WriteLine($"Garbage collection occurred {GC.CollectionCount(0)} times");
    ReadLine();
}
```

All that this does is return the result and then output the number of times that the garbage collection has taken place.

Take note that I have added using static System.Console to my using statements. This allows me to drop the Console before the WriteLine and ReadLine methods.

Running the application now produces the following result.

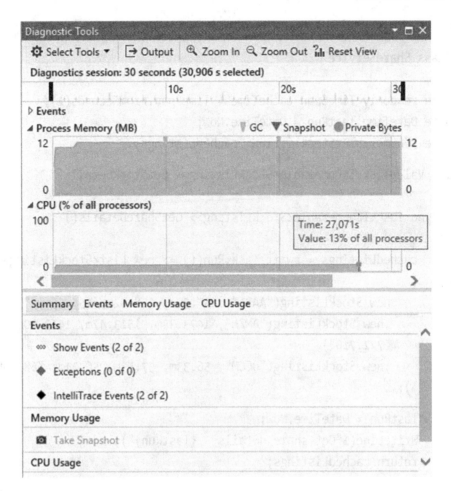

Figure 1-14. *Task<T> diagnostic results*

The following is evident from the diagnostic tools:

- Process memory is around 12MB.

- The time it took to complete the process was 27,071 seconds.

The output to the console application screen also reported that garbage collection occurred 1833 times in generation 0. Let's go and improve the code in the ShareService class and make use of the ValueTask type.

Listing 1-44. Improved ShareService class

```
public class ShareService
{
    private readonly TimeSpan cacheTime = TimeSpan.FromSeconds(2);
    private DateTime lastRun = DateTime.Now;
    private IEnumerable<StockListing> cachedListings;

    public ValueTask<IEnumerable<StockListing>> GetStockDetails()
    {
        async Task<IEnumerable<StockListing>> GetShareDetails()
        {
            cachedListings = await Task.Run(() => new List<StockListing>
            {
                new StockListing("AAPL", 157.50m, 158.52m, 154.55m, "741,37B")
                ,new StockListing("AMZN", 1473.35m, 1513.47m, 1449.00m,
                "722,71B")
                ,new StockListing("QCOM", 56.33m, 57.53m, 56.24m, "68,86B")
            });

            lastRun = DateTime.Now;
            WriteLine($"Get share details - {lastRun}");
            return cachedListings;
        }

        if (DateTime.Now - lastRun < cacheTime)
        {
            return new ValueTask<IEnumerable<StockListing>>(cachedListings);
        }

        return new ValueTask<IEnumerable<StockListing>>(GetShareDetails());
    }
}
```

You will notice that I have replaced Task<IEnumerable<StockListing>> with
ValueTask<IEnumerable<StockListing>> and I have also removed the async keyword.
It makes sense to remove the async keyword, because most of the time the results will
be returned synchronously. Running the application a second time using the improved
code produces the following improved results.

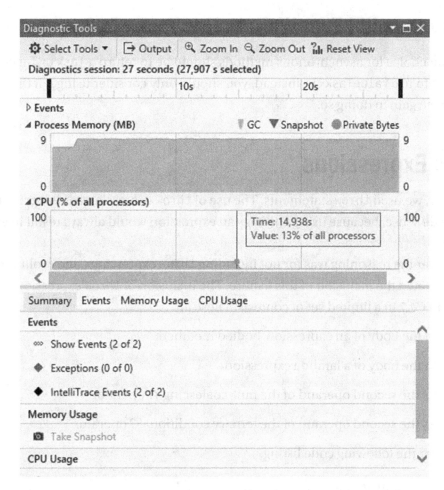

Figure 1-15. *ValueTask<T> diagnostic results*

The following information is now evident from the diagnostic tools, and there is definitely an improvement:

- Process memory is around 9MB (down from 12MB).

- The time it took to complete the process was 14,938 seconds (down from 27,071 seconds on the previous run).

The output to the console application screen also reported that garbage collection occurred 0 times in generation 0.

ValueTask is a value type. This means that by returning the cached stock listings, no allocations occurred on the heap.

So Why Should I Ever Want to Use Task<T>?

The default choice for asynchronous methods should be to return a Task or Task<T>. If you want to use ValueTask<T> instead, you should only consider using it if there is a performance gain in doing so.

Throw Expressions

Before C# 7, we used throw statements. The use of throw expressions didn't exist. It sort of made sense, because using throw as an expression would always result in an exception.

Whatever the reasoning was for not including throw expressions, the evolution of C# has necessitated the inclusion of this feature. The inclusion of throw expressions is now available in C# 7 in a limited set of contexts. These are

- In the body of an expression-bodied members

- In the body of a lambda expression

- As the second operand of the null-coalescing ?? operator

- As the second operand of the ternary conditional ? operator

Consider the following code listing.

Listing 1-45. Null check in constructor

```
public class Square
{
    public int Side { get; }
    public string Description { get; }
    public Square(int side, string description)
    {
        if (description == null)
        {
            throw new ArgumentNullException(nameof(description));
        }

        Side = side;
```

```
        Description = description;
    }
}
```

Visual Studio now proposes a code improvement for us, because we can use a throw expression here to simplify the code.

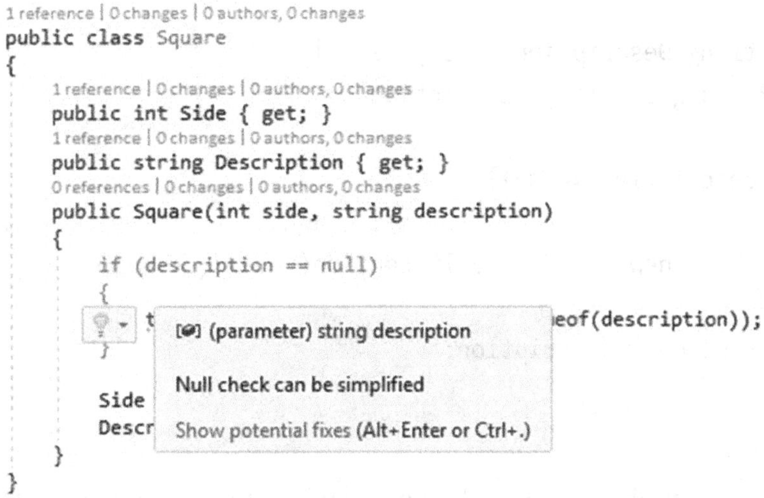

Figure 1-16. *Visual Studio proposes simplified code*

Clicking the lightbulb will suggest using a throw expression instead. The code is therefore refactored to look as follows.

Listing 1-46. Null check extension method

```
public class Square
{
    public int Side { get; }
    public string Description { get; }
    public Square(int side, string description)
    {
        Side = side;
        Description = description ?? throw new ArgumentNullException
        (nameof(description));
    }
}
```

With the advent of expression-bodied members that extend to constructors in C# 7, we are able to simplify code even more when we are dealing with a constructor that can be changed to an expression body definition. Consider this code.

Listing 1-47. A simple constructor

```
public class Rectangle
{
    public string Description { get; set; }
    public Rectangle(string description)
    {
        if (description == null)
        {
            throw new ArgumentNullException(nameof(description));
        }
        Description = description;
    }
}
```

Because we can apply expression-bodied members to constructors and because throw expressions are available to expression-bodied members, we can greatly simplify the code as follows.

Listing 1-48. Expression-bodied constructor

```
public class Rectangle
{
    public string Description { get; set; }
    public Rectangle(string description) => Description = description ??
    throw new ArgumentNullException(nameof(description));
}
```

The constructor of our Rectangle class has been reduced to a single line of code. Throw expressions are a necessary part of C# as it has evolved to what we have today. Using throw expressions will not only make your code easier to understand but also reduce the amount of code you have to write.

Discards

As I pointed out earlier, during the discussion of out parameters, C# 7 saw the introduction of discards. This is a really welcome addition to the language. It allows you to tell the compiler that you do not care about the value of a specific variable. Discards are therefore dummy or temporary variables that are not going to be used at all in your application.

It therefore also makes sense that discards are unassigned and do not contain a value, which in turn reduces memory allocations. To indicate that a variable is a discard, you use the underscore _ as the variable name.

Take note that int _ for example is still a valid variable name and can therefore not be used in the same scope as a discard.

Discards are supported in the following contexts:

- Tuples

- Pattern matching

- Out parameters

- Standalone as _ when no other _ is in scope

Also note that when a discard is used, you can't read its value or use it in an assignment. Remember that we mentioned earlier that a discard variable is not assigned a value at all. Let's have a look at a few use cases.

Tuples

Previously in the chapter, we had a look at how to use tuples in C# 7. What we learned was that tuples are a great way to return multiple values from a single method call. We also had a look at local functions. You will remember that sometimes code has logic that is only relevant to its enclosing method. In other words, it does not make sense to put the code contained inside the local function in a standalone public method.

Let us have a look now at a usage scenario where we combine these two features of C# 7 and then enhance it by using discards. The code example is a local function that checks to see if a given value is greater than zero and less than 20. It is then flagged as being in range. Consider the following code.

Listing 1-49. Using tuples without discards

```
private void UsingDiscards()
{
    // Local function
    (bool zeroCheck, bool maxCheck, bool inRangeCheck) DoSomething(int value)
    {
        bool blnAboveZero = false;
        bool blnBelowTwenty = false;
        bool blnInRange = false;
        if (value > 0)
            blnAboveZero = true;
        if (value <= 20)
            blnBelowTwenty = true;
        if (blnAboveZero && blnBelowTwenty)
            blnInRange = true;
        return (blnAboveZero, blnBelowTwenty, blnInRange);
    }

    var (isZero, isNotmax, inRange) = DoSomething(15);
}
```

The local function returns a tuple that has three Boolean variables for the above zero check, the below 20 check, and the flag to mark the value as being in range or not.

Strictly speaking, the local function's inRangeCheck value is good enough to tell us that both the zero check and the max value check are true. I can therefore change the code as follows.

Listing 1-50. Using discards in tuples

```
private void UsingDiscards()
{
    // Local function
    (bool zeroCheck, bool maxCheck, bool inRangeCheck) DoSomething(int value)
    {
        bool blnAboveZero = false;
        bool blnBelowTwenty = false;
        bool blnInRange = false;
```

```
        if (value > 0)
            blnAboveZero = true;
        if (value <= 20)
            blnBelowTwenty = true;
        if (blnAboveZero && blnBelowTwenty)
            blnInRange = true;
        return (blnAboveZero, blnBelowTwenty, blnInRange);
    }

    var (_, _, blnValid) = DoSomething(15);
}
```

We can therefore just discard the zero check and max check values by using _ in the deconstruction. In doing so, I am telling the compiler that I do not care what the first two check values are of the variables returned by the tuple.

Out Parameters

The enhancements to out parameters in C# 7 are quite welcome. Earlier in the chapter, we had a look at how to use out parameters. What is clear is that we no longer need to declare a standalone variable when using out parameters. This was quite evident when we created the TryParse.

Note that out parameters are not only useful as the out parameter of a TryParse. It can also add a lot of value when used in regular methods when you want a single additional value back and using a tuple is somewhat of an overkill.

In TryParse specifically, the out parameter can be somewhat useless in some instances. Discards provide a neat solution to this problem. Consider the following code listing.

Listing 1-51. Using out parameters with discards

```
// Out parameters
if (bool.TryParse("true", out _))
    Debug.WriteLine("The string value is a valid boolean");
else
    Debug.WriteLine("The string value is not a valid boolean");
```

I'm not going to be using the out parameter at all. All I want to do is check if the value is a valid Boolean or not. I can therefore tell the compiler that I do not care for the out parameter and that it can be discarded.

Standalone Discard

The discard can be used standalone to indicate that you want to ignore the variable. You might be wondering when this is useful. Consider the following call to the ExecuteCommand method.

Please note that the SQL query and SQL Connection String parameters are just placeholders. You will need to add valid values here, otherwise the code will throw an exception.

By default, it returns the number of rows affected by an UPDATE, INSERT, or DELETE statement.

Listing 1-52. Standalone discard variable

```
private void UsingDiscards()
{
    // Standalone discard
    _ = ExecuteCommand("[UPDATE table SQL]", "[sql connection string here]");
}

private int ExecuteCommand(string sql, string sqlConnectionString)
{
    using (SqlConnection conn = new SqlConnection(sqlConnectionString))
    {
        SqlCommand cmd = new SqlCommand(sql, conn);
        cmd.Connection.Open();
        return cmd.ExecuteNonQuery();
    }
}
```

In the call to the ExecuteCommand method, I used a discard variable to ignore the number of rows affected. I know that using ExecuteCommand("[UPDATE table SQL]", "[sql connection string here]"); without a variable assignment doesn't return anything (obviously), but I wanted to illustrate that using a discard variable _ essentially does the same thing.

Another example would be to choose to ignore the Task object returned from the async DoSomethingAsync method in the following console application code listing.

Listing 1-53. Ignoring the Task object returned with discard

```
public static async Task DoSomethingAsync(int valueA, int valueB)
{
    WriteLine("Async started at: " + DateTime.Now);
    _ = Task.Run(() => valueA + valueB);

    await Task.Delay(5000);
    WriteLine("Async completed at: " + DateTime.Now);
}
```

Discards can be very beneficial if you want to improve your code readability and the performance of your application. Admittedly, the reduced memory allocation from using a single discard variable will most likely be small. For large applications, ignoring unnecessary variables could make quite a difference indeed.

Pattern Matching

If you think back to the section on pattern matching, you will remember that we used an is expression to check if we were working with a Student, Lecturer, Alumnus, or ExchangeStudent object.

Discards can be used with is expressions too. Consider the following code listing.

Listing 1-54. Using discard with is expression

```
// Using discard with is expression
if (someperson is Student student)
{
    return $"{student.StudentDetails().fullName} is enrolled for {student.
    StudentDetails().studentCourse} with student number {student.
    StudentDetails().studentNum}";
```

```
}
else if (someperson is Lecturer lecturer)
{
    return $"{lecturer.LecturerDetails().fullName} teaches {lecturer.
    LecturerDetails().courseSpecial}";
}
else if (someperson is Alumnus alumnus)
{
    return $"{alumnus.AlumnusDetails().fullName} has completed {alumnus.
    AlumnusDetails().degreeObtained} in {alumnus.AlumnusDetails().
    yearCompleted}";
}
else if (someperson is ExchangeStudent exchStudent)
{
    return $"{exchStudent.ExchangeStudentDetails().fullName} has
    {exchStudent.ExchangeStudentDetails().daysLeftOnVisa} days left on
    Student Visa";
}
else if (someperson is var _)
{
    return $"Invalid {nameof(someperson)} object passed.";
}
```

The last statement basically says that if I can't match the class to anything, then I don't really know what I am dealing with. Assigning a variable here would not make sense really, so I just use the discard variable and return a message to the calling code.

We can do exactly the same with a switch statement.

Listing 1-55. Using discard with a switch

```
// Using discard with switch
switch (someperson)
{
    case Student student:
        return $"{student.StudentDetails().fullName}";
    case Lecturer lecturer:
        return $"{lecturer.LecturerDetails().fullName}";
```

```
    case Alumnus alumnus:
        return $"{alumnus.AlumnusDetails().fullName}";
    case ExchangeStudent exchangeStudent:
        return $"{exchangeStudent.ExchangeStudentDetails().fullName}";
    case var _:
        return $"Invalid {nameof(someperson)} object passed.";
}
```

The same reasoning is true for switches. If I don't know what I am dealing with, I can use a discard variable to return a message to the calling code to indicate that the parameter passed didn't match any of the expected objects.

Wrapping Up

We have gone through quite a few features of C# 7. We started off with looking at tuples and how to change the default positional names for the tuple values. We also had a look at comparing tuples and how tuples can infer tuple element names.

We then took a look at pattern matching and how to use the is type pattern and the switch pattern. We also saw how to use when clauses in case expressions as well as checking for null.

The next section was a short look at out variables where I introduced discards and discussed this briefly in the context of out variables.

Local functions were next and I showed you how this can benefit you when the code you are using in your local function only applies to the containing member.

With generalized async return types, we saw that it definitely can improve the performance of your application when used correctly. You will remember that the suggested course of action is to use Task or Task<T> and that only after doing performance testing should you consider using ValueTask<T>.

Throw expressions were then discussed, and you learned that the evolution of C# necessitated the use of throw expressions in certain circumstances.

Lastly, we revisited discards in more detail as it pertained to tuples, out parameters, pattern matching, and standalone discards.

CHAPTER 2

Exploring C#

This chapter will have a look at some of the features in C# that developers might overlook. This is a statement I hear all too often when discussing a specific feature: "I've heard of it but not used it before."

Features such as abstract classes and interfaces. Do you know what the difference is between the two and how you would use one over the other? How about lambda expressions? Have you used this feature before in your everyday coding?

This chapter is all about exploring C# a little further. We will not be discussing C# 7 specific code, but rather features of the C# language in general. The following topics will be discussed:

- Using and implementing abstract classes

- Using and implementing interfaces

- Asynchronous programming using async and await

- Making use of extension methods

- Generics

- Nullable type

- Dynamic type

Discussing the features of C# would be incomplete without a brief tour of the history of the language. Let's see how it all began.

The History of C#

In January 1999, Anders Hejlsberg and his team started building this new language called *Cool*. It stood for *C-like Object Oriented Language* but was renamed to C# by the time the Professional Developers Conference was held in July 2000.

© Dirk Strauss 2019
D. Strauss, *Exploring Advanced Features in C#*, https://doi.org/10.1007/978-1-4842-4856-0_2

It has been stated that the decision to change the name from *Cool* to C# was due to certain trademark restrictions. Microsoft began work on finding another name, but one that still had a reference to C.

As you know, the ++ operator in C# is used to increment a variable by 1. Seeing as there was already a language called C++, the team at Microsoft needed to come up with something different, but similar. Calling it C++++ would not work, but if you look at the four + symbols, the # symbol can be seen as four + symbols strung together.

This meant that the next increment of this C-like Object Oriented Language would be called C#. The reference to music is also interesting, especially when one considers that the # is a musical notation that raises a note a semitone higher. Table 2-1 lists the versions of C# as well as the features released in those versions.

Table 2-1. *C# Through the Years*

C# Version	Release Date	.NET Framework	Visual Studio	Feature Overview
C# 1.0	Jan 2002	1.0	VS 2002	Classes, structs, interfaces, events, properties, delegates, expressions, statements, attributes, literals
C# 1.2	Apr 2003	1.1	VS 2003	Small enhancements, foreach loops now called Dispose on IEnumerator when it implemented IDisposable
C# 2.0	Nov 2005	2.0	VS 2005	Generics, partial types, anonymous methods, nullable types, iterators, covariance and contravariance. Enhancements to existing features such as separate accessibility for getter and setters, static classes, delegate interface
C# 3.0	Nov 2007	3.0 and 3.5	VS 2008	Auto-implemented properties, anonymous types, query expressions, lambda expressions, expression trees, extension methods, implicitly typed local variables, partial methods, object and collection initializers

(continued)

Table 2-1. (*continued*)

C# Version	Release Date	.NET Framework	Visual Studio	Feature Overview
C# 4.0	Apr 2010	4	VS 2010	Dynamic binding, names/optional arguments, generic covariant and contravariant, embedded interop types
C# 5.0	Aug 2012	4.5	VS 2012 VS 2013	Asynchronous members (async and await), caller info attributes
C# 6.0	Jul 2015	4.6	VS 2015	Static imports, exception filters, auto-property initializers, expression-bodied members, null propagator, string interpolation, nameof operator, index initializers, await in catch/finally, default values for getter-only properties
C# 7.0	Mar 2017	4.6.2	VS 2017	Out variables, tuples, discards, pattern matching, local functions, throw expressions, generalized async and return types, literal syntax improvements, ref locals and returns, more expression-bodied members
C# 7.1	Aug 2017	4.7	VS 2017	Async Main method, default literal expressions, inferred tuple element names
C# 7.2	Nov 2017	4.7.1	VS 2017	Conditional ref expressions, private protected access modifier, leading underscores in numeric literals, non-trailing named arguments, techniques for writing safe efficient code
C# 7.3	May 2018	4.7.2	VS 2017	Reassign ref local variables, initializers on stackalloc arrays, using fixed statement with any type that supports a pattern, testing tuple types with == and !=, using expression variables in more locations

For more information on the features of the different releases of C#, refer to the Microsoft documentation at `https://docs.microsoft.com`.

Now that we have seen where we have come from, let's look at some of the specific features of C# as outlined at the beginning of the chapter.

Using and Implementing Abstract Classes

Before we can have a look at abstract classes, we first need to take a look at the `abstract` modifier and what that means. The `abstract` modifier simply tells you that the thing that is being modified does not have a complete implementation. This modifier can be used with

- Classes

- Methods

- Properties

- Indexers

- Events

When we use the `abstract` modifier in a class declaration, we are actually saying that the class we are creating is only the basic base class of other classes.

This means that any members marked as abstract or that are included in the base class have to be implemented by the derived classes (classes that use the base class). You will also hear that abstract classes are also referred to as blueprints.

Abstract Class Features

Abstract classes therefore have the following important features:

- You cannot create an instance of an abstract class.

- An abstract class can contain abstract methods and accessors.

- You cannot use the `sealed` modifier with abstract classes.

- If a non-abstract class is derived from an abstract class, the derived class has to include the implementations of the abstract methods and accessors.

The reason that the `sealed` modifier cannot be used with an abstract class is because the `sealed` modifier prevents class inheritance while the abstract modifier requires that a class must be inherited.

Abstract Methods

The use of the `abstract` modifier in a method or property declaration simply states

- The abstract method is implicitly a virtual method.

- You can only use abstract methods in abstract classes.

- Abstract methods have no implementation; therefore it has no method body.

- You are not allowed to use the `static` or `virtual` modifiers in an abstract method declaration.

What do we mean when we say that an abstract method has no implementation and therefore no method body? Consider the following code listing.

Listing 2-1. Abstract method declaration

```
public abstract void MyAbstractMethod();
```

This basically tells us that the derived class needs to implement this method and provide the implementation for this method.

Abstract Properties

When thinking about abstract methods, you will notice that abstract properties behave in quite a similar way. The real difference is in the declaration and invocation syntax:

- You cannot use the `abstract` modifier on a static property.

- You can override the inherited abstract property in the derived class by declaring a property that uses the `override` modifier.

All this will make more sense when looking at some code examples. Let's illustrate the use of abstract classes next.

Using Abstract Classes

To illustrate the use of abstract classes, I will create a very simplistic abstract class. It will then be inherited and used in a derived class. Consider the following listing.

Listing 2-2. Abstract class

```
abstract class AbstractBaseClass
{
    protected int _propA = 100;
    protected int _propB = 200;
    public abstract int PropA { get; }
    public abstract int PropB { get; }
    public abstract int PerformCalculationAB();
}
```

Now that we have our abstract class, let's go and instantiate it. As Figure 2-1 shows us, we have an error. Why would we have an error?

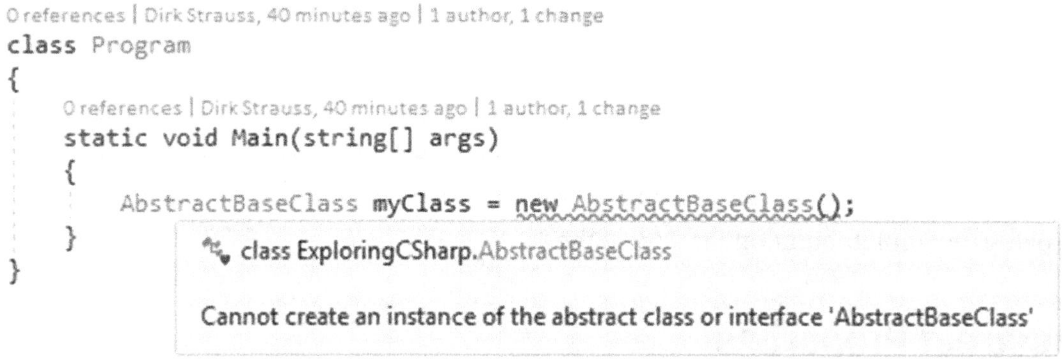

Figure 2-1. *Error on abstract class instantiation*

Aha! Remember that I stated earlier that we cannot instantiate an abstract class. The compiler displays an error stating that you cannot create an instance of an abstract class. We can however create a new class and derive it from the abstract class. Consider the following code listing.

Listing 2-3. Inheriting from an abstract class

```
class DerivedClass : AbstractBaseClass
{

}
```

We inherit from the abstract class in the derived class called `DerivedClass`. The compiler then gives us another warning as seen in Figure 2-2.

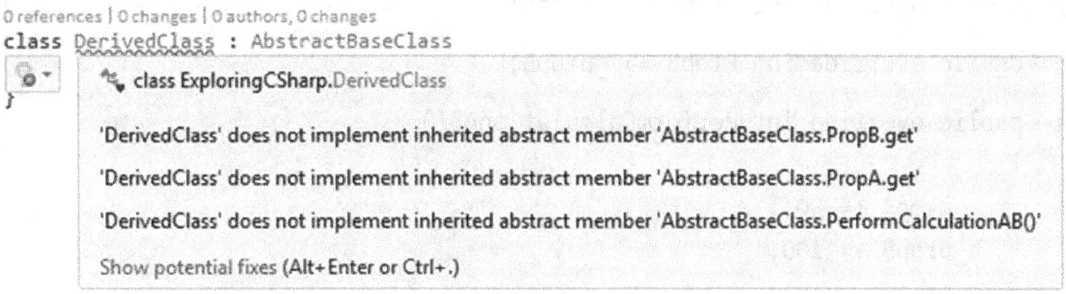

Figure 2-2. *Derived class implementations*

The compiler is telling you that you need to implement the members of the abstract class. Visual Studio will automatically be able to provide the implementation structure for you when you click the lightbulb and click *Implement Abstract Class*. After doing this, your code will look as in Listing 2-4.

Listing 2-4. Implementing the abstract class

```
class DerivedClass : AbstractBaseClass
{
    public override int PropA => throw new NotImplementedException();

    public override int PropB => throw new NotImplementedException();

    public override int PerformCalculationAB()
    {
        throw new NotImplementedException();
    }
}
```

You will notice that the generated code will throw a NotImplementedException. This makes sense because you haven't actually provided any implementation for the code and the compiler cannot guess what you want to do in your derived class. Let's add some code to our derived class as seen in Listing 2-5.

Listing 2-5. Code implementation added

```
class DerivedClass : AbstractBaseClass
{
    public override int PropA => _propA;

    public override int PropB => _propB;

    public override int PerformCalculationAB()
    {
        _propA += 50;
        _propB += 100;

        return _propA + _propB;
    }
}
```

In the calling code, we can now instantiate the derived class and write out the values.

For this I simply used a console application that added using static System. Console; to the using statements.

Listing 2-6. Calling the derived class

```
static void Main(string[] args)
{
    DerivedClass d = new DerivedClass();
    WriteLine($"PropA before calculation {d.PropA}");
    WriteLine($"PropB before calculation {d.PropB}");
    WriteLine($"Perform calculation {d.PerformCalculationAB()}");
    WriteLine($"PropA after calculation {d.PropA}");
    WriteLine($"PropB after calculation {d.PropB}");
    ReadLine();
}
```

Inspecting the output of the code we wrote, you will see that the default values for the two properties are displayed. After performing the calculation, our property values have changed.

Listing 2-7. Output from code in derived class

```
PropA before calculation 100
PropB before calculation 200
Perform calculation 450
PropA after calculation 150
PropB after calculation 300
```

The output of the console application is not critical here. What I wanted to show you is a working example of a derived class that inherits from the abstract class you created earlier.

When Do I Use an Abstract Class?

The code listings in the preceding section are a bit abstract (pun intended). Why not just define a class as normal? When should you use an abstract class?

This is something that I think many developers might ponder, but the logic for using abstract classes is quite simple once you understand a fundamental concept.

An abstract class acts like a common noun that describes the derived objects. This is clearly illustrated when we consider the following description.

Sedan, SUV, pickup, and hatchback are all vehicles. Even though a sedan is quite different from an SUV or a pickup, they all share the commonality of being vehicles.

Vehicles therefore must have an engine, a VIN, headlights, and so on. These (and many more) would be the common traits between vehicles. We can therefore declare an abstract class called Vehicle and give it these common traits that the derived classes (the sedan, SUV, etc.) must implement.

It is therefore up to the derived class to add implementation to the abstract class and then have additional properties and methods specific to the derived class only. For example, the pickup will have a loading bay that the sedan will not have. A sedan will have a boot space.

While this example is rather simplistic, it illustrates the concept really well. A more real-world example would be an ERP system that uses sales orders and purchase orders. These are both orders, and we can define an abstract class called `Order` that defines an order number, order status, order line count, and so on.

The derived classes `SalesOrder` and `PurchaseOrder` must both have these properties, but only a sales order can have customer information while a purchase order will contain supplier information.

Abstract classes therefore allow us to clearly define the commonality between closely related derived objects.

Using and Implementing Interfaces

In the previous section, we had a look at abstract classes. You will remember that I said that abstract classes act like a common noun that describes the derived objects. When referring to interfaces however, we are talking about the fact that interfaces contain definitions that group related functionality. This means that the classes or structs that implement an interface share a common bit of functionality.

Think back to our abstract class example of a vehicle. We said that cars, SUVs, etc. are all vehicles. Therefore, the abstract `Vehicle` class tells us what common traits the derived classes must implement. When referring to interfaces however, we are saying that some or all of the derived classes share some sort of functionality. We can thus think of interfaces as verbs that describe an action.

Let us assume that all vehicles must have a VIN. This is something that we can use to check that no two vehicles have the same VIN.

A VIN is a unique vehicle identification number used in the automotive industry to identify motor vehicles.

It is therefore safe to say that we can create an interface called `IComparable` that will add the ability of comparing vehicle VINs. Then, we know that different vehicles have different features. Usually the more you spend on a vehicle, the more features they have. There are however certain features that only make sense on certain vehicles. A differential lock (or difflock) is something that would only make sense on certain vehicles such as an SUV.

We can therefore safely say that creating an interface called `IDiffLockable` will add the ability to determine if certain vehicles can have an automatic difflock or not.

Take note that by convention interfaces are usually created with names beginning with an I.

Interfaces have the following properties:

- It's like an abstract class; therefore any class or struct implementing an interface must implement its members.

- You cannot directly instantiate an interface.

- Interface members are implemented by the class or struct that does the implementation.

- Events, indexers, properties, and methods can all be contained in an interface.

- Interfaces contain no implementation of methods.

- You are allowed to implement multiple interfaces on a class or struct.

- You are allowed to inherit from a base class and also implement multiple interfaces.

Let us go ahead and create the two interfaces for our vehicle classes and take a closer look at how we will use these interfaces.

Creating the Abstract and Derived Classes

Let us go ahead and create an abstract class called `Vehicle` from which our derived classes will inherit.

Listing 2-8. The Vehicle abstract class

```
abstract class Vehicle
{
    protected int _wheelCount = 4;
    protected int _engineSize = 0;
```

```
    protected string _vinNumber = "";
    public abstract string VinNumber { get; }
    public abstract int EngineSize { get; }
    public abstract int WheelCount { get; }
}
```

This abstract class is rather simplistic in nature, but its purpose is to provide the members for implementation to the deriving classes called Car and SUV that we will create.

Listing 2-9. Car class

```
class Car : Vehicle
{
    public override string VinNumber => _vinNumber;

    public override int EngineSize => _engineSize;

    public override int WheelCount => _wheelCount;

    public Car(string vinNumber, int engineSize, int wheelCount)
    {
        _vinNumber = vinNumber;
        _engineSize = engineSize;
        _wheelCount = wheelCount;
    }
}
```

Listing 2-10. SUV class

```
class SUV : Vehicle
{
    public override string VinNumber => _vinNumber;

    public override int EngineSize => _engineSize;

    public override int WheelCount => _wheelCount;

    public SUV(string vinNumber, int engineSize, int wheelCount)
    {
```

```
        _vinNumber = vinNumber;
        _engineSize = engineSize;
        _wheelCount = wheelCount;
    }
}
```

Now that we have created the abstract Vehicle class and the derived Car and SUV classes, we can go ahead and create our interfaces.

Creating the Interfaces

As mentioned earlier, we need to be able to compare the VINs of vehicles to ensure that they are indeed unique numbers. For this purpose, we will be creating an IComparable interface by using the interface keyword.

Listing 2-11. IComparable interface

```
interface IComparable<T>
{
    bool VinNumberEqual(T obj);
}
```

This interface will therefore require any class or struct that implements this interface to provide a definition for a method called VinNumberEqual that matched the signature specified by the interface.

You will notice the use of the *T* type parameter in the IComparable interface. We are working with a generic interface here, where the client code decides what type of object we are comparing. This chapter discusses Generics later on.

In other words, any class that implements IComparable must contain a method called VinNumberEqual. We also want to be able to specify if a vehicle has an automatic difflock feature. For this, we will create an interface called IDiffLockable.

Listing 2-12. IDiffLockable interface

```
interface IDiffLockable
{
    bool AutomaticDiff { get; }
}
```

The same logic is therefore true with this interface. Implementing classes must provide a property called AutomaticDiff that will enable or remove that feature from a vehicle.

Implementing the Interfaces

We will now implement the IComparable interface on the Car class. The Car class already inherits from the Vehicle abstract class. In order to implement IComparable, we need to add it as follows.

Listing 2-13. Implementing IComparable

```
class Car : Vehicle, IComparable<Car>
```

Visual Studio will now prompt you to implement the IComparable interface as can be seen in Figure 2-3.

Figure 2-3. *Visual Studio prompt to implement interface*

When you click the lightbulb and implement the interface, your code will look as follows.

Listing 2-14. IComparable interface implemented on Car class

```
class Car : Vehicle, IComparable<Car>
{
    public override string VinNumber => _vinNumber;
```

```
    public override int EngineSize => _engineSize;

    public override int WheelCount => _wheelCount;

    public Car(string vinNumber, int engineSize, int wheelCount)
    {
        _vinNumber = vinNumber;
        _engineSize = engineSize;
        _wheelCount = wheelCount;
    }

    public bool VinNumberEqual(Car car)
    {
        return VinNumber.Equals(car.VinNumber);
    }
}
```

The interface member VinNumberEqual is added to your class and defaults to throw a NotImplementedException. To implement the interface method, add some code to return a Boolean if the Car objects are equal. This allows us to check if the VIN of two vehicles are equal by using the following code.

Listing 2-15. Checking the VIN of two Car classes

```
Car car1 = new Car("VIN12345", 2, 4);
Car car2 = new Car("VIN12345", 2, 4);
WriteLine(car1.VinNumberEqual(car2) ? "ERROR: Vin numbers equal" : "Vin
numbers unique");
```

This simple example shows us how we can use an interface to add functionality to a class, because classes and structs must implement the interface members.

But what about the SUV class? It needs to implement the IComparable and IDiffLockable interfaces. We do this as follows.

Listing 2-16. Implementing IComparable and IDiffLockable

```
class SUV : Vehicle, IComparable<SUV>, IDiffLockable
{

}
```

Visual Studio now also prompts you to implement the interfaces on the SUV class. When we have done this and added your implemented code, your class will look as follows.

Listing 2-17. SUV class with implemented interfaces

```
class SUV : Vehicle, IComparable<SUV>, IDiffLockable
{
    public override string VinNumber => _vinNumber;

    public override int EngineSize => _engineSize;

    public override int WheelCount => _wheelCount;

    public bool AutomaticDiff { get; } = false;

    public SUV(string vinNumber, int engineSize, int wheelCount, bool autoDiff)
    {
        _vinNumber = vinNumber;
        _engineSize = engineSize;
        _wheelCount = wheelCount;
        AutomaticDiff = autoDiff;
    }

    public bool VinNumberEqual(SUV suv)
    {
        return VinNumber.Equals(suv.VinNumber);
    }
}
```

We are implementing the VIN check and the automatic difflock feature.

Sometimes we will have a situation where two interfaces have the same method, but with different implementations. This can easily lead to an incorrect implementation of one or both of the interfaces. It is for this reason that we are able to explicitly implement an interface member.

Being able to use interfaces allows you to extend the functionality of several classes from a single interface. The thing of using an interface is that it could apply to one or more (but not all) classes. This is evident in the fact that only IDiffLockable was implemented on the SUV class, while IComparable was implemented on both the Car and SUV classes.

Asynchronous Programming Using Async and Await

Asynchronous programming will allow you to write code that can perform long running tasks while still keeping your application responsive. With the introduction of async in the .NET Framework 4.5, it eased the previously complicated approach to implementing asynchronous functionality in your applications.

In this section, we will have a look at how to use async and await and how these can benefit your development efforts.

How Do I Write Async Methods?

To write async methods, the use of the `async` and `await` keywords is necessary. The following points are the typical characteristics of asynchronous methods:

- The method signature must include the `async` modifier.

- The method must return `Task<T>`, `Task`, `void`, or `ValueTask<T>`.

- The method statements must include at least one `await` expression.

- By convention, your method names should end with *Async*.

To illustrate the concept of async code, you will create a Windows Forms project that reads a large file and counts the lines it reads as it processes each line of text in the file.

For this purpose, I downloaded a large text file containing the text of War and Peace. I then copied that text a few times to create a very large text file.

Our application will process the file and update a label on the UI to notify the user how many lines have been read. Throughout this process, the application will remain totally responsive.

The basic form design (Figure 2-4) includes a label for keeping track of the current lines counted and another label that will display the total lines read once the process has completed. It also has a button that is used to start the file read.

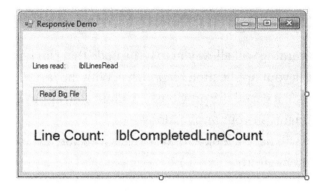

Figure 2-4. *Responsive form design*

In the code behind, you will add an async method called ReadFileAsync. It is here that we will add our async file read logic.

Listing 2-18. ReadFileAsync async method

```
private async Task<int> ReadFileAsync()
{
    var FileLines = new List<string>();
    int lineCount = 0;
    using (var reader = File.OpenText(@"C:\temp\big_file.txt"))
    {
        string line = string.Empty;
        while ((line = await reader.ReadLineAsync().ConfigureAwait(false))
        != null)
        {
            FileLines.Add(line);
            lineCount += 1;

            if (lblLinesRead.InvokeRequired)
            {
                lblLinesRead.Invoke(new Action(() => lblLinesRead.Text =
                lineCount.ToString()));
            }
            else
            {
                lblLinesRead.Text = lineCount.ToString();
```

```
            }
        }
    }

    return lineCount;
}
```

You will notice that I use the `InvokeRequired` method on the label control to update the text property because we are on a different thread than the one the label control was created on. If you try to update the text property on the label here without using `InvokeRequired`, you will receive a cross-thread violation error.

Next you need to change the button click event to be async and call the await on the ReadFileAsync method. The code will look as follows.

Listing 2-19. Button click event

```
private async void btnReadBigFile_Click(object sender, EventArgs e)
{
    int linesInFile = await ReadFileAsync();
    lblCompletedLineCount.Text = linesInFile.ToString();
}
```

Run your application and click the *Read Big File* button (Figure 2-5) to start the file read process. Notice that you can move your Windows Form around and resize it throughout the file read process.

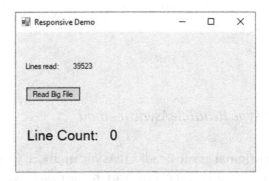

Figure 2-5. *Responsive file read application*

The *Line Count* label will only be updated at the completion of the file read process. This is great, and we have a really simple async method. But what is happening in the background? What is the compiler doing to make this all work?

Under the Hood

Let us go ahead and use a decompiler to see the generated code for our async ReadFileAsync method.

I am using a trial version of Redgate's .NET Reflector to have a look at the compiler generated code.

```
1 reference | 0 changes | 0 authors, 0 changes
private async Task<int> ReadFileAsync()
{
    var FileLines = new List<string>();
    int lineCount = 0;

    using (var reader = File.OpenText(@"C:\temp\big_file.txt"))
    {
        string line = string.Empty;
        while ((line = await reader.ReadLineAsync().ConfigureAwait(false)) != null)
        {

            FileLines.Add(line);
            lineCount += 1;

            if (lblLinesRead.InvokeRequired)
            {
                lblLinesRead.Invoke(new Action(() => lblLinesRead.Text = lineCount.ToString()));
            }
            else
            {
                lblLinesRead.Text = lineCount.ToString();
            }
        }
    }

    return lineCount;
}
```

Figure 2-6. *Original async ReadFileAsync method*

Looking back at our original async ReadFileAsync method, you will notice that it is actually a pretty straightforward code (Figure 2-6). It conforms to the characteristics of async methods as detailed earlier.

Listing 2-20. Compiler generated code for the async ReadFileAsync method

```
[CompilerGenerated]
private sealed class <ReadFileAsync>d_ 3 : |AsyncStateMachine
{
    // Fields
     public int <>1_state;
     public AsyncTaskMethodBuilder<int> <>t_builder;
     public Form1 <>4_ this;
     private Form1.<>c_DisplayClass3_0 <>8_1;
     private List<string> <FileLines>5_2;
     private StreamReader <reader>5_3;
     private string <line>5_4;
     private string <>s_5;
     private ConfiguredTaskAwaitable< string>.ConfiguredTaskAwaiter <>u_1;

    // Methods
    public <ReadFileAsync>d_3();
    private void MoveNext();
    [DebuggerHidden]
    private void SetStateMachine(|AsyncStateMachine stateMachine);
}
```

The code generated by the compiler however is a totally different beast. As a start, the compiler actually generates a class. In the original code, we created a method. Here we see that the compiler has created a sealed class that implements the IAsyncStateMachine interface.

Then, all the variables in the ReadFileAsync method are now fields in the sealed class. This means that the variables we created in the method are captured as fields in the state machine which is used to manage the local state. If our ReadFileAsync method had been passed a parameter, it too would be captured as a field in the sealed class.

Having a look further down, you will notice a method called MoveNext. The state machine is coded into a MoveNext which is called for each step. This tracks an Integer state with a variable called num and uses it to execute code.

Therefore, each time our code calls await, there will be another state and MoveNext that manages the state of our async method.

Listing 2-21. MoveNext method for state machine

```csharp
private void MoveNext()
{
    int num = this.<>1__state;
    try
    {
        if (num != 0)
        {
            this.<>8__1 = new Form1.<>c_DisplayClass3_0();
            this.<>8__1.<>4_this = this.<>4__this;
            this.<FileLines>5__2 = new List<string>();
            this.<>8__1.lineCount = 0;
            this.<reader>5__3 = File.OpenText(@"C:\temp\big_file.txt");
        }
        try
        {
            ConfiguredTaskAwaitable<string>.ConfiguredTaskAwaiter awaiter;
            if (num == 0)
            {
                awaiter = this.<>u__1;
                this.<>u__1 = new ConfiguredTaskAwaitable<string>.
                ConfiguredTaskAwaiter();
                this.<>1__state = num = -1;
            }
            else
            {
                this.<line>5__4 = string.Empty;
                goto TR_0014;
            }
        TR_0010:
            this.<>s__5 = awaiter.GetResult();
            if ((this.<line>5__4 = this.<>s__5) != null)
            {
                this.<FileLines>5__2.Add(this.<line>5__4);
                this.<>8__1.lineCount++;
```

```
    if (!this.<>4__this.lblLinesRead.InvokeRequired)
    {
        this.<>4__this.lblLinesRead.Text = this.<>8__1.
        lineCount.ToString();
    }
    else
    {
        Action method = this.<>8__1.<>9__0;
        if (this.<>8__1.<>9__0 == null)
        {
            Action local1 = this.<> 8__1.<>9__0;
            method = this.<>8__1.<>9__0 = new Action(this.<>
            8__1.<ReadFileAsync>b__0);
        }
        this.<>4__this.lblLinesRead.Invoke(method);
    }
    goto TR_0014;
}
else
{
    this.<>s__5 = null;
    this.<line>5__4 = null;
}
goto TR_0003;
TR_0014:
    while (true)
    {
        awaiter = this.<reader>5__3.ReadLineAsync().
        ConfigureAwait(false).GetAwaiter();
        if (awaiter.IsCompleted)
        {
            goto TR_0010;
        }
        else
        {
```

```
                this.<>1__state = num = 0;
                this.<>u__1 = awaiter;
                Form1.<ReadFileAsync>d__3 stateMachine = this;
    this.<>t__builder.AwaitUnsafeOnCompleted<ConfiguredTaskAwaitable<string>.
    Configured
            }
            break;
        }
        return;
    }
    finally
    {
        if ((num < 0) && (this.<reader>5__3 != null))
        {
            this.<reader>5__3.Dispose();
        }
    }
  TR_0003:
    this.<reader>5__3 = null;
    int lineCount = this.<>8__1.lineCount;
    this.<>1__state = -2;
    this.<>t_builder.SetResult(lineCount);
  }
  catch (Exception exception)
  {
    this.<>1__state = -2;
    this.<>t_builder.SetException(exception);
  }
}
```

The whole MoveNext method is wrapped in a try / catch block. This means that even if your async method does not have a try / catch handler, any exceptions are still caught. This is how await is able to re-throw exceptions in the calling code.

Some Final Tips

The topic of async and await is very big, and there is a lot to learn. Most of this learning will be done by writing the code and making the mistakes. Here are a few tips that might help ease the learning curve.

Avoid Using Wait()

It is generally considered best practice to avoid the use of Wait in the following situation. Look at the following pseudo code listing.

Listing 2-22. Using Wait

```
async Task PerformSomeLongRunningOperation()
{
    DoSomeWork(false).Wait();
}

async Task DoSomeWork(bool blnToggleIsOn)
{
    // Some work is done here
}
```

In our async PerformSomeLongRunningOperation method, we have a call to DoSomeWork that passes a Boolean as parameter and calls Wait. Doing this gives us no benefit of using async and await, because the Wait is blocking code.

Because the DoSomeWork async method is returning a Task, we should use await. Our code then needs to change as follows.

Listing 2-23. Using await

```
async Task PerformSomeLongRunningOperation()
{
    await DoSomeWork(false);
}
```

If we had to run the DoSomeWork async method synchronously for whatever reason, we need to make use of GetAwaiter and GetResult as in the following code listing.

Listing 2-24. Using GetAwaiter and GetResult

```
async Task PerformSomeLongRunningOperation()
{
    DoSomeWork(false).GetAwaiter().GetResult();
}
```

Essentially GetAwaiter GetResult do the same thing as Wait (which is block), but the only difference is that GetAwaiter GetResult will unwrap any exceptions thrown inside the DoSomeWork method.

Use ConfigureAwait(false) When Necessary

When working with Windows Form applications, the application uses a UI thread. This means that the context is a UI context. The same is true for a web application. When responding to ASP.NET requests, the context is an ASP.NET request context. If neither UI nor request context is used, the thread pool is used.

If your code is not touching the UI, then using ConfigureAwait(false) tells the async method not to resume on the context. It will then resume on a thread in the thread pool. If it is set to true, then the code attempts to marshal the continuation back to the original context.

Making Use of Extension Methods

Since C# 3.0, extension methods have been making a huge difference in how I use my code. I am able to add methods to existing types without creating a new derived type. The C# Programming Guide describes extension methods as a special kind of static method. The only difference is that they are called as if they were instance methods on the type being extended (i.e., called by using instance method syntax).

But what exactly is a useful extension method? Let us have a look at an example of an extension method.

Checking If a String Is a Valid Integer

The example I will use is quite a simple one. You are going to check if a string value is a valid Integer. You start off by creating a static class that contains your static extension method.

Take note that the first argument in the parentheses is a reference to what is being extended. In other words, this String refers to the type that this extension method acts on. It acts on strings.

That is really all there is to this extension method. It takes the value of the type being extended and checks to see if it can be parsed as an integer. A true or false is then returned to the calling code. Consider the following code listing.

Listing 2-25. Extension method example

```
public static class ExtensionMethods
{
    public static bool IsValidInt(this String value)
    {
        bool blnValidInt = false;
        if (int.TryParse(value, out int result))
        {
            blnValidInt = true;
        }
        return blnValidInt;
    }
}
```

When calling the extension method IsValidInt on a string variable, you will notice that the Intellisense labels it as a square with a down arrow (Figure 2-7). This denotes an extension method in the Intellisense window. Hitting *Alt+X* while the Intellisense window is open will show only extension methods. What is surprising is just how many extension methods there are.

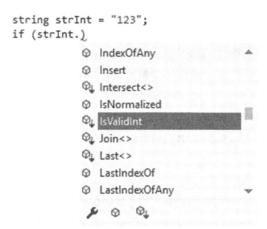

```
string strInt = "123";
if (strInt.)
```

Figure 2-7. *Extension method Intellisense*

Another thing to notice is that because you specified that the extension method only extends string types, it will obviously not be available on other types such as Boolean, etc. You did this by adding this String value to the extension method arguments.

If you wanted this extension method to extend another type, you need to specify this in the signature of the extension method.

Listing 2-26. Calling IsValidInt

```
string strInt = "123";
if (strInt.IsValidInt())
{
    WriteLine("Valid Integer");
}
else
{
    WriteLine("Not an Integer");
}
```

You can also pass additional arguments to an extension method. In the next example, we want to return the integer value if it is a valid Integer. This can easily be done with an out parameter as follows.

Listing 2-27. Passing argument to an extension method

```
public static bool IsValidInt(this String value, out int integerValue)
{
    bool blnValidInt = false;
    integerValue = 0;
    if (int.TryParse(value, out int result))
    {
        blnValidInt = true;
        integerValue = result;
    }
    return blnValidInt;
}
```

This allows you to be very flexible with your usage of extension methods.

Extension Methods Are Lower Priority Than Instance Methods

One thing to take note of though is that extension methods have a lower priority than instance methods defined in the type itself. Extension methods will extend a class or interface, but won't override them.

The compiler will always look for a match in the type's instance methods when encountering a method invocation. Thereafter, it will search for any extension methods defined for the type.

From time to time, you might see an error that states that a type does not contain a definition for a method you invoked and that no accessible extension method accepting that type as a first argument could be found. This is the compiler trying to find what you invoked, but can't. It is also interesting that extension methods are mentioned last.

This is best illustrated with an example. Go ahead and create the following class.

Listing 2-28. Class with DoSomething method

```
public class WorkerClass
{
    public void DoSomething()
    {
        Console.WriteLine("I am a method of the WorkerClass");
    }
}
```

Next, create an extension method called DoSomething.

Listing 2-29. Extension method DoSomething

```
public static void DoSomething(this Car value)
{
    Console.WriteLine("I am an extension method");
}
```

Creating an instance of the class and running the code will display the text *I am a method of the WorkerClass.*

Listing 2-30. Calling the DoSomething method

```
WorkerClass worker = new WorkerClass();
worker.DoSomething();
```

This means that the extension method will never be called because the DoSomething method of the class has a higher priority than the extension method, and the signatures of both methods are the same.

If you had to change the signature of the DoSomething extension method, the extension method will be called. Consider the following code listing.

Listing 2-31. DoSomething method with changed signature

```
public static void DoSomething(this WorkerClass value, int iValue)
{
    Console.WriteLine($"I am an extension method with parameter {iValue}");
}
```

If you called the extension method with `worker.DoSomething(5);` the console application will output the text *I am an extension method with parameter 5*. This is because the signatures of the `DoSomething` method on the class and the `DoSomething` extension method are different.

Generics

Generics have been with us since C# 2. The goal was to allow developers to reuse code while maintaining type safety. Think of generics as a blueprint that will allow you to define data structures that are type safe without the commitment of actually defining a type.

With generics, the calling code decides the type when instantiating a generic class, for example. You will see later on that the generic class we create will allow a mix of types to be collected.

You might not know it, but you have actually been using generics all along. Generics are used in LINQ, Lists (Figure 2-8), Dictionaries, and so on. The code inside these structures is focused on managing the code without having to worry about the type.

```
List<>

List<T>
Represents a strongly typed list of objects that can be accessed by index.
T: The type of elements in the list.
```

Figure 2-8. *List of T*

Think back to when you create a `List<>`. This uses generics and allows you to specify the type when you create that list. You can create a list of integers just as easily as creating a list of doubles or a list of your own custom classes.

By convention, T is used in generics to denote that something uses a generic type parameter.

When creating a generic class, we can give it a generic type parameter that looks as follows.

Listing 2-32. VehicleCarrier of T

```
public class VehicleCarrier<T>
```

The T is used between angle brackets, and you can define more than one type parameter. T is therefore used as a parameter of your class definition. We can also say that T parametizes the types you will use inside the class.

You can do the same with arrays.

Listing 2-33. Array of T

```
private T[] _loadbay;
```

Instead of defining an array of integers, you define an array of T. If used inside my class, T will be the type passed to the class in the type parameter.

Non-generic VehicleCarrier Class

Let me illustrate the benefit of using generics. In the following code listing, I have a class that is used to hold a collection of Car objects.

Think of the vehicle carrier trucks used in the motor industry to transport vehicles.

In my VehicleCarrier class, I have a _capacity that just allows me to add a specific number of Car objects to the _loadbay array. I can't add more vehicles than the maximum number defined in the capacity variable.

Listing 2-34. Non-generic VehicleCarrier class

```
public class VehicleCarrier
{
    private Car[] _loadbay;
    private int _capacity;

    public VehicleCarrier(int capacity)
    {
        _loadbay = new Car[capacity];
        _capacity = capacity;
    }

    public void AddVehicle(Car vehicle)
    {
```

```
        var loaded = _loadbay.Where(x => x != null).Count();
        if (loaded == _capacity)
        {
            Console.WriteLine($"Vehicle Carrier filled to capacity
            {_capacity}.");
        }
        else
        {
            _loadbay[loaded] = vehicle;
        }
    }

    public void GetAllVehicles()
    {
        foreach (Car vehicle in _loadbay)
        {
            Console.WriteLine($"Vehicle with VIN number {vehicle.VinNumber}
            loaded");
        }
    }
}
```

All that this VehicleCarrier class does is contain the collection of cars and passes that around to other places in my code. When I need to inspect the carrier, I can output all the VINs of the cars contained in the VehicleCarrier class. In order to use this class, I can create a few Car objects and add these to a list.

Note, as mentioned earlier, you are already using generics here by using a List of T in your code. In this situation, you are creating a List of Car.

This list is then added to my VehicleCarrier class in a foreach.

Listing 2-35. Using non-generic VehicleCarrier class

```
//Without Generics
Car car1 = new Car("123", 2, 4);
```

```
Car car2 = new Car("456", 3, 4);
Car car3 = new Car("789", 2, 4);

List<Car> carList = new List<Car>(new Car[] { car1, car2, car3 });

VehicleCarrier carrier = new VehicleCarrier(3);
foreach (var vehicle in carList)
{
    carrier.AddVehicle(vehicle);
}

carrier.GetAllVehicles();
```

When I call the GetAllVehicles method, the output of the class is simply the VINs of each Car object contained in the VehicleCarrier class.

Listing 2-36. Console window output from non-generic VehicleCarrier class

```
Vehicle with VIN number 123 loaded
Vehicle with VIN number 456 loaded
Vehicle with VIN number 789 loaded
```

The VehicleCarrier class (Figure 2-9) is a great way to collect and move Car objects around, but unfortunately, I can only use it with Car objects.

```
SUV suv1 = new SUV("123", 2, 4, false);
SUV suv2 = new SUV("456", 3, 4, false);
SUV suv3 = new SUV("789", 2, 4, false);


List<SUV> carList = new List<SUV>(new SUV[] { suv1, suv2, suv3 });

VehicleCarrier carrier = new VehicleCarrier(3);
foreach (var vehicle in carList)
{
    carrier.AddVehicle(vehicle);
}

carrier.GetAllVehicles(
```

> [●] (local variable) SUV vehicle
>
> Argument 1: cannot convert from 'ExploringCSharp.SUV' to 'ExploringCSharp.Car'
>
> Show potential fixes (Alt+Enter or Ctrl+.)

Figure 2-9. *Error*

I would not be able to use my VehicleCarrier class to transport SUV objects. Doing so would result in a compiler error. Our VehicleCarrier class is therefore very limiting in its functionality. We can't be flexible in its use, because it only accepts Car objects.

Changing VehicleCarrier Class to Be Generic

Let's make a few changes to the VehicleCarrier class in order to make it more flexible. I will start off by adding a generic type parameter to my class. Here I am telling the compiler that my class will use a type of T.

I am now able to define my _loadbay as an array of T. In fact, throughout my VehicleCarrier class, I can replace the type Car with T.

The following code listing is the modified VehicleCarrier class and also contains a jazzed-up GetAllVehicles method that uses pattern matching.

Listing 2-37. Generic VehicleCarrier class

```
public class VehicleCarrier<T>
{
    private T[] _loadbay;
    private int _capacity;

    public VehicleCarrier(int capacity)
    {
        _loadbay = new T[capacity];
        _capacity = capacity;
    }

    public void AddVehicle(T vehicle)
    {
        var loaded = _loadbay.Where(x => x != null).Count();
        if (loaded == _capacity)
        {
            Console.WriteLine($"Vehicle Carrier filled to capacity
            {_capacity}.");
        }
        else
        {
```

```csharp
                _loadbay[loaded] = vehicle;
        }
    }

    public void GetAllVehicles()
    {
        foreach (T vehicle in _loadbay)
        {
            switch (vehicle)
            {
                case Car car:
                    Console.WriteLine($"{car.GetType().Name} with VIN
                    number {car.VinNumber} loaded");
                    break;
                case SUV suv:
                    Console.WriteLine($"{suv.GetType().Name} with VIN
                    number {suv.VinNumber} loaded");
                    break;
                default:
                    Console.WriteLine($"Vehicle not determined");
                    break;
            }
        }
    }
}
```

This allows me to create a list of SUV objects and pass that to my VehicleCarrier
class. I am no longer constrained to only using Car objects in my VehicleCarrier class.

Listing 2-38. Using generic VehicleCarrier class

```csharp
// With Generics
SUV suv1 = new SUV("123", 2, 4, false);
SUV suv2 = new SUV("456", 3, 4, false);
SUV suv3 = new SUV("789", 2, 4, false);

List<SUV> carList = new List<SUV>(new SUV[] { suv1, suv2, suv3 });
```

```
VehicleCarrier<SUV> carrier = new VehicleCarrier<SUV>(3);
foreach (var vehicle in carList)
{
    carrier.AddVehicle(vehicle);
}

carrier.GetAllVehicles();
```

Calling the method GetAllVehicles returns the VINs of the SUV objects contained in my class.

Listing 2-39. Console window output from generic VehicleCarrier class

```
SUV with VIN number 123 loaded
SUV with VIN number 456 loaded
SUV with VIN number 789 loaded
```

This means that I am free to create a VehicleCarrier of Car and a VehicleCarrier of SUV using the same VehicleCarrier class. See the benefit?

Mix and Match

I am also able to mix and match by specifying that my VehicleCarrier class is used with the type object. This allows me to create a List of Car and SUV objects and add that to my VehicleCarrier class.

Listing 2-40. Loading SUV and Car classes

```
SUV suv1 = new SUV("123", 2, 4, false);
Car car1 = new Car("456", 3, 4);
SUV suv3 = new SUV("789", 2, 4, false);

List<object> carList = new List<object>(new object[] { suv1, car1, suv3 });

VehicleCarrier<object> carrier = new VehicleCarrier<object>(3);
foreach (var vehicle in carList)
{
    carrier.AddVehicle(vehicle);
}

carrier.GetAllVehicles();
```

I am now able to call the `GetAllVehicles` method that uses the switch statement and pattern matching to output the VIN of the specific object it is dealing with.

Listing 2-41. Generic VehicleCarrier class of object output

```
SUV with VIN number 123 loaded
Car with VIN number 456 loaded
SUV with VIN number 789 loaded
```

My generic `VehicleCarrier` of T is now totally generic and performant. It cuts down on code duplication and allows me more flexibility in my application.

Recap and More on Generics

When we end a class with angle brackets <> we call it a generic class. Generics, however, do not stop there. We can also have generic structs, generic interfaces, and generic delegates. As mentioned earlier, the T represents the type parameter. It defines what type of data a generic class (for example) will be working with.

T is just a convention used, but you can use any name you wish. Sticking to the convention of T is probably a good idea anyway.

T is therefore like a placeholder that can be used throughout the class in places that we need to define types. This can be on fields, local variables, parameters passed to methods, or return types from methods.

The calling code using a generic class is therefore responsible for defining the type that will be used throughout the class by passing the type parameter. In our example this was the `VehicleCarrier<Car>` portion of the code.

Generics and Collections

Collections in C# manage and organize data. You are definitely aware of List, and if you remember earlier, we saw that a List is generic. We can therefore think of a List as follows.

Listing 2-42. List of T

```
public class List<T>
{
    public void Add(T listItem);
}
```

We need to know when to use which collection to manage our data. This will make sense if we want to be as efficient as possible. Here is a summary of the generic collections and their uses.

List<T>

The List<T> holds a collection of data types. When the list's capacity is reached, it doubles the capacity to accommodate more data. The List<T> can therefore grow as needed.

Queue<T>

Think of the Queue<T> as a queue you would be standing in, inside of a bank. You might get a little upset if someone comes into the bank after you, but gets assisted before you. This is because you were first and have been waiting longer. Queue<T> is exactly the same. It provides the Enqueue method to queue items and a Dequeue method to remove the items in the order they were added in. We call this *First In First Out* or a FIFO collection.

Stack<T>

When thinking of Stack<T> imagine a can of Pringles crisps. The crisp you see first when opening the lid is the last crisp added to the can. The same is true for Stack<T>, because it uses *Last In First Out* or LIFO. To accomplish this, it exposes the methods Push and Pop. You push an item onto the stack and pop it off the stack from the top.

HashSet<T>

If you require a collection to only contain unique items, you can use a HashSet<T>. It will only allow unique items. In order to do this, the Add method returns a true or a false if the add was successful or not. A HashSet<T> works well with value types. It is, however, not too good with objects and reference types unless you create an instance of an object and add that.

LinkedList<T>

The LinkedList<T> will give you more control over managing the items in the Linked List. It does this by exposing a Next and a Previous method. It also provides flexible inserts with methods such as AddFirst, AddLast, AddBefore, and AddAfter.

Dictionary<TKey, TValue>

This is another collection that you might be used to working with. Dictionaries provide quick lookups of data by using a key. A Dictionary therefore has a Key and a Value that we call the key-value pair.

SortedDictionary<TKey, TValue>

If you need to have a sorted collection of data, then consider the SortedDictionary<TKey, TValue>. This generic collection knows how to sort the data it contains right out of the box. Items are sorted by key. If your key is a string, then it will sort your data alphabetically. You need to use a sorted dictionary if you are looking up things often. It is optimized for addition and removal of data.

SortedList<TKey, TValue>

If you need an efficient generic collection that also provides items stored within it as sorted, consider using a SortedList<TKey, TValue>. A sorted list is optimized to use the least amount of memory possible.

SortedSet<T>

If you need a sorted collection that only allows unique items, you will need to use a SortedSet<T>. Like the HashSet<T> we looked at earlier, it only allows unique items, but sorted in order.

Generic Interfaces

Generics also allow you to create generic interfaces. You will remember in the section on interfaces that we created an IComparable generic interface. This time, we will create an interface to define what the VehicleCarrier class does. This is useful if we need to create other types of carriers that differ slightly in functionality.

Imagine for a minute that we need a vehicle carrier that can dynamically add vehicles and does not have a fixed capacity. Based on the previous section on *Generics and Collections*, you might remember that a List<T> can help us here. Our generic interface will look as follows.

Listing 2-43. Generic ICarrier interface

```
public interface ICarrier<T>
{
    void AddVehicle(T value);
    void GetAllVehicles();
}
```

You will notice that the generic interface also takes a generic type parameter. Here we are saying that this interface must require any class that implements it to have a GetAllVehicles method and an AddVehicle method that accepts a value of T. Now we are able to modify our existing VehicleCarrier class to implement ICarrier<T>.

Listing 2-44. Modifying VehicleCarrier class

```
public class VehicleCarrier<T> : ICarrier<T>
{

}
```

We can also create a new DynamicCarrier class that will resize its capacity as more vehicles are added to it. Consider the following code.

Listing 2-45. DynamicCarrier<T> class implements ICarrier<T>

```
public class DynamicCarrier<T> : ICarrier<T>
{
    private List<T> _loadbay;

    public DynamicCarrier()
    {
        _loadbay = new List<T>();
    }
```

```csharp
public void AddVehicle(T vehicle)
{
    _loadbay.Add(vehicle);
}

public void GetAllVehicles()
{
    foreach (T vehicle in _loadbay)
    {
        switch (vehicle)
        {
            case Car car:
                Console.WriteLine($"{car.GetType().Name} with VIN
                number {car.VinNumber} loaded");
                break;
            case SUV suv:
                Console.WriteLine($"{suv.GetType().Name} with VIN
                number {suv.VinNumber} loaded");
                break;
            default:
                Console.WriteLine($"Vehicle not determined");
                break;
        }
    }
}
}
```

Because DynamicCarrier<T> implements ICarrier<T>, it must have the AddVehicle and GetAllVehicles methods. I am now free to add logic to all classes that implement ICarrier<T>, simply by adding to the interface itself. While VehicleCarrier<T> and DynamicCarrier<T> both serve the same purpose (to transport vehicles), the logic contained inside each is quite different.

For a recap on interfaces, refer to the section on interfaces at the beginning of this chapter.

Nullable Type

In C#, all reference types such as strings and program-defined objects are nullable. In fact, null is the default value of reference type variables. This means that while they can be null, we actually need to see the null keyword as a literal that represents a null reference. Put differently, something that does not refer to any object in .NET Framework.

With the release of C# 2.0, we were introduced to nullable value types. If you have a look at the System.Nullable namespace (Figure 2-10), you will notice that we are dealing with a generic type here.

```
System.Nullable<|
    Nullable<T> where T : struct
    Represents a value type that can be assigned null.
    T: The underlying value type of the Nullable<T> generic type.
```

Figure 2-10. *System.Nullable<T>*

This means that we can now create a Nullable<int> and assign any Integer value from MinValue to MaxValue to it including null. The same is true for the rest of the value types.

Some Characteristics of Nullable Types

The following is true when we talk about nullable types in C#:

- Because reference types already support null, nullable types only apply to value types.

- Nullable<T> can also be referred to as T?

- Because the value types can be nullable, you can use the HasValue readonly property to test for null and then use the readonly Value property to get its value.

- You can use the == and != operators with nullable types.

- C# 7.0 allows the use of pattern matching to check for null and get the value.

- You can use the null-coalescing operator to check for null, and if null, assign a value to the underlying type.

While we have defined what nullable types are, how exactly do we use them? More importantly, why should we use them? Well sometimes you might expect a null to be assigned to a value type in certain circumstances. Being able to define a value type as nullable allows you to write better and safer code. Consider the following code listings.

Using Nullable Types

In the following figure (Figure 2-11), you will see that I can assign a value to the iValue integer as well as the nullable iValue2 integer. Trying to assign null to the iValue3 integer gives me a compiler error.

```
// Valid code
int iValue = 10;
int? iValue2 = 10;

// iValue3 not valid
int iValue3 = null;
int? iValue4 = null;
```

Figure 2-11. *iValue4 nullable type allows null*

Consider the following logic when using a nullable value type of int. It checks to see if the iValue2 variable has a value and, if so, assigns the value to the variable iValue.

Listing 2-46. Checking a nullable type with HasValue

```
// Valid code
int iValue = 10;
int? iValue2 = null;

if (iValue2.HasValue)
{
    iValue = iValue2.Value;
}
else
{
    iValue = -1;
}
```

In the preceding code listing, the console application will return a -1 because the value of the iValue2 variable is null. Using the null-coalescing operator, we can simplify the code tremendously by writing the preceding code block as follows.

Listing 2-47. Using a null-coalescing operator

```
int? iValue2 = null;
int iValue = iValue2 ?? -1;
```

How snazzy is that? Our code has been reduced to two lines of code, and it does exactly the same thing as in Listing 2-46. With C# 7.0 we are now able to use pattern matching too. We can therefore do the following.

Listing 2-48. Use pattern matching

```
int iValue = 10;
int? iValue2 = null;
if (iValue2 is int value)
{
    iValue = value;
}
else
{
    iValue = -1;
}
```

If the variable iValue2 is null (which in this case it is), the application will return -1. If, however, the value is not null, the variable iValue will be set to the value of iValue2.

A Peek Inside Nullable<T>

In the preceding sections, we had a look at some characteristics of Nullable<T> and how to use Nullable<T>. But what actually makes it (for lack of a better word) tick?

Peeking under the hood, we see that Nullable<T> is a struct (Figure 2-12). We also see the expected HasValue and Value properties discussed previously.

```
namespace System
{
    public struct Nullable<T> where T : struct
    {
        public Nullable(T value);

        public bool HasValue { get; }
        public T Value { get; }

        public override bool Equals(object other);
        public override int GetHashCode();
        public T GetValueOrDefault();
        public T GetValueOrDefault(T defaultValue);
        public override string ToString();

        public static implicit operator T? (T value);
        public static explicit operator T(T? value);
    }
}
```

Figure 2-12. *Under the hood of Nullable<T>*

Furthermore, you will notice the GetValueOrDefault method we often see when working with LINQ. From the image in Figure 2-12, you will notice that it is an overloaded method.

You can retrieve the value of the current Nullable<T> object or you can provide a default value if my Nullable<T> object is indeed null. But what happens if the Nullable<T> object is null but you do not provide a default value?

In that case, the default value of the underlying type is returned. To demonstrate this, consider the following code.

Listing 2-49. GetValueOrDefault

```
int iValue = 10;
int? iValue2 = null;
iValue = iValue2.GetValueOrDefault(-1);
WriteLine($"The value of iValue = {iValue}");
```

This code in Listing 2-49 will return the default value we provide which is -1. We are providing it the default value that needs to be returned if the Nullable<T> object is indeed null. Now remove the default value and run the code again.

Listing 2-50. Default value of the underlying type

```
int iValue = 10;
int? iValue2 = null;
iValue = iValue2.GetValueOrDefault();
WriteLine($"The value of iValue = {iValue}");
```

The code in Listing 2-50 will return the default value of the underlying type. Because the underlying type is an integer, the default value is 0. Table 2-2 shows the default values of value types.

Table 2-2. *Default Values of Value Types*

Default	Value Type
0	int, byte, sbyte, short, uint, ulong, ushort
false	bool
'\0'	char
0M	decimal
0.0D	double
0.0F	float
0L	long

The default value of a struct would be produced by setting all the value type fields to the default values of that specific type and setting all the reference type fields to null.

Starting with C# 7.1, you can use the default literal expression to initialize a variable with the default value specific to its type.

Listing 2-51. Using the default literal

```
bool? blnValue = default;
int? iVal = default;
double? dblValue = default;
decimal? decVal = default;
```

```
WriteLine($"The default values are " +
    $"- blnValue = {blnValue.GetValueOrDefault()} " +
    $"- iVal = {iVal.GetValueOrDefault()} " +
    $"- dblValue = {dblValue.GetValueOrDefault()} " +
    $"- decVal = {decVal.GetValueOrDefault()}");

ReadLine();
```

The use of nullable types in C# definitely provides some benefit to you as a developer. Being able to provide the underlying type with a default value also makes it really easy to avoid surprises. This is especially true when working with data coming out of a database.

Dynamic Type

With the release of C# 4.0, developers were introduced to a new dynamic type. It's a static type, but dynamic objects bypass static type checking. Think of it acting like it has a type object. It is best explained with some code examples.

Listing 2-52. The dynamic type

```
dynamic dObject = "I am dynamic";
WriteLine($"dObject = {dObject}");

dObject = 1;
WriteLine($"dObject = {dObject}");

dObject = false;
WriteLine($"dObject = {dObject}");

dObject = 1.1;
WriteLine($"dObject = {dObject}");
```

The compiler does not know what type the variable is at compile time. It is also quite logical then that there is no IntelliSense available on a dynamic type. Therefore, the type of the dynamic variable will be determined at runtime. The code in Listing 2-52 will produce the following output.

Listing 2-53. Dynamic output

```
dObject = I am dynamic
dObject = 1
dObject = False
dObject = 1,1
```

As you can imagine, pattern matching works rather well with dynamic variables. It can be a simple if (dObject is int iValue) {} or a more elaborate case statement.

Listing 2-54. Pattern matching with dynamic variable

```
switch (dObject)
{
    case int iObject:
        WriteLine($"dObject is an Integer {iObject}");
        break;
    case bool blnObject:
        WriteLine($"dObject is a bool {blnObject}");
        break;
    case string strObject:
        WriteLine($"dObject is a string {strObject}");
        break;
    case double dblObject:
        WriteLine($"dObject is a double {dblObject}");
        break;
    default:
        WriteLine($"dObject type can't be determined");
        break;
}
```

It is interesting to note that the dynamic type only exists at compile time. At runtime, the dynamic type variables are compiled into variables of type object.

You are allowed to use dynamic in

- Fields

- Properties

- Parameters

- Return types

- Local variables

You are also allowed to use dynamic as the target type of a conversion. Consider the following code listing.

Listing 2-55. Conversion to dynamic

```
dynamic dObj;
bool blnFalse = false;
dObj = (dynamic)blnFalse;

WriteLine($"dObj = {dObj}");
```

A new API called the *dynamic language runtime (DLR)* was added to the .NET Framework 4. This API supports the dynamic type in C# and also the implementation of dynamic programming languages, e.g., IronRuby.

Wrapping Up

C# is a language that has grown a lot in the past couple of years. With C# 7 we have seen quicker point releases that introduced new features and improvements that you can use in your day-to-day development.

As a developer, it remains a challenge to stay up to date with what is new. Microsoft has a fantastic resource in the form of online documentation at https://docs.microsoft.com.

This chapter can never be complete because there is so much in the C# language that it needs to cover. The limits of trying to do so in a single chapter are evident in the page count. We had a look at abstract classes and what interfaces are. We then looked at async and await and how these can help you create responsive applications. We also saw how async and await work the magic they do by taking a peek at the state machine it creates.

I then illustrated the use of extension methods and what this feature can do for your development. We also saw that generics play a big role in C# and that you have most likely been using generics all along (think of List<T>).

Lastly, we took a slightly deeper dive into Nullable<T> and how it fits together as well as a brief explanation of the dynamic type. In the next chapter, we will be taking a look at the new features of C# 8.0.

CHAPTER 3

The New Features of C# 8.0

The design process of C# is open source. You can head over to the repository at `https://github.com/dotnet/csharplang` and have a look at some of the discussions surrounding the language design. In fact, the *meetings* documents make for fascinating reading.

Once you are in the GitHub repo, have a look at dotnet/csharplang/meetings for a collection of documents organized by year.

The first thing that strikes me as obvious is that the thinking surrounding the C# language is very structured and deliberate. All throughout the repository, you will see that the last commit date is always quite recent. This therefore proves that the repository you are looking at is a living document that you can follow along with and stay up to date with.

What about C# 8.0? Well the truth is that even as the C# team released the incremental point releases for C# 7 (C# 7.1 to C# 7.3), they were also working on C# 8.0.

This chapter will have a look at the following new features in C# 8.0:

- Nullable reference types

- Recursive patterns

- Ranges and indices

- Switch expressions

- Target-typed new expressions

- Async streams

- Using declarations

© Dirk Strauss 2019
D. Strauss, *Exploring Advanced Features in C#*, https://doi.org/10.1007/978-1-4842-4856-0_3

In order to follow along in code with the code listings I will illustrate in this chapter, you will need a copy of Visual Studio 2019. At the time of writing this chapter, Visual Studio 2019 Preview (Version 16.0.0 Preview 2.0) was available for download.

Make sure that if you are using the Preview of Visual Studio 2019, you have selected C# 8.0 (beta) from the *Advanced Build Settings* (Figure 3-1). To do this, right-click the project and select *Properties*. Then select the *Build* tab and then click the *Advanced* button.

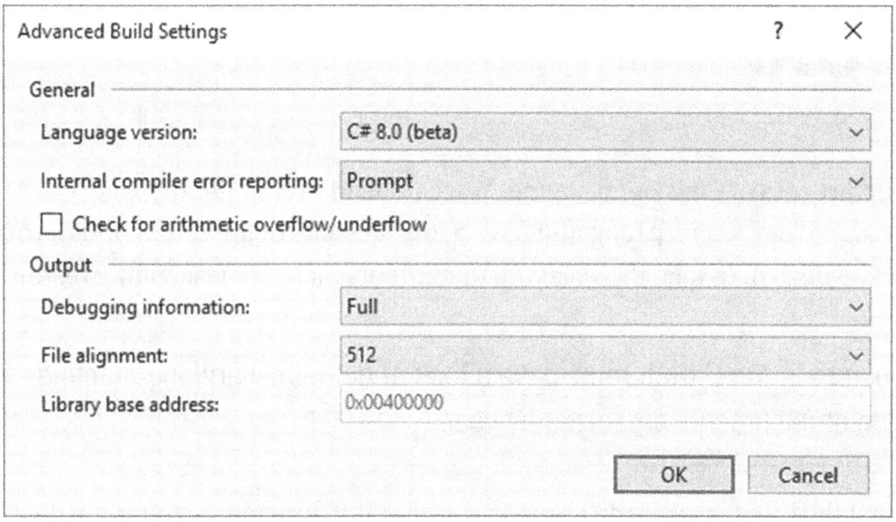

Figure 3-1. *Advanced Build Settings*

Please note that some of the features illustrated in the following text might contain slight variations between this preview and the final release of C# 8.0. At the time of writing this book, the code in this chapter was syntactically correct.

To kick things off, let's start looking at what nullable reference types are.

Nullable Reference Types

If you think back to Chapter 2, we discussed nullable types. We said that all reference types such as strings are nullable and that the default value of reference types is null. With the release of C# 2.0, Microsoft introduced nullable value types.

I am not going to rehash the difference between reference types and value types. I will leave that up to you to read up about if you're unsure. The fact that reference types can now be nullable is something that (in my opinion) developers have needed for a long time. The thinking behind making reference types nullable is to help developers avoid NullReferenceException exceptions.

You will remember from the previous chapter that in order to mark a variable as nullable, you need to use the type and ? when declaring a variable. For example, int? represents a nullable int. Now you can do the same with reference types such as string? to declare a nullable string.

What is great about this addition is that you can now express your design intent more clearly. I can say that some variables could have a value while others must have a value.

Enabling Nullable Reference Types

This feature is not enabled by default in C# 8.0. You have to opt into the nullable reference types feature even if you are creating C# 8.0 applications. With the nullable reference types feature switched on, all your reference variable declarations will become *non-nullable* reference types. Therefore, you need to take note of this when enabling nullable reference types.

Even with nullable reference types enabled, Visual Studio will only display a warning when encountering a non-nullable reference type set to null.

This means that if you create a reference type (a string variable declaration, for example) without enabling nullable reference types, you will not see any warnings. Consider the following.

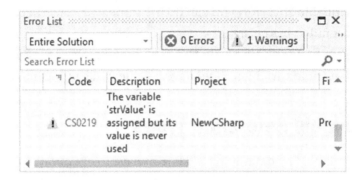

```
0 references | Dirk Strauss, 23 hours ago | 1 author, 1 change
class Program
{
    0 references | Dirk Strauss, 23 hours ago | 1 author, 1 change
    static void Main(string[] args)
    {
        string strValue = null;
    }
}
```

Figure 3-2. *No nullable reference type warning*

The warning displayed in Figure 3-2 is the *variable assigned but never used* warning. To enable the nullable reference types feature in your applications, you need to add a new pragma #nullable enable anywhere in your source file. This will turn on the nullable reference types feature.

```
0 references | Dirk Strauss, 23 hours ago | 1 author, 1 change
class Program
{
    #nullable enable
    0 references | Dirk Strauss, 23 hours ago | 1 author, 1 change
    static void Main(string[] args)
    {
        string strValue = null;
    }
}
```

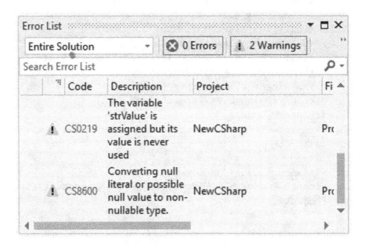

Figure 3-3. *Nullable reference types turned on*

The warning is displayed in the *Error List* (Figure 3-3). If you enable this feature on an existing project, you might encounter a few of these warnings.

The pragma #nullable enable also supports disable to turn off the nullable reference types feature.

If you need to enable nullable reference types for your entire project, open your .csproj file and look for the LangVersion element.

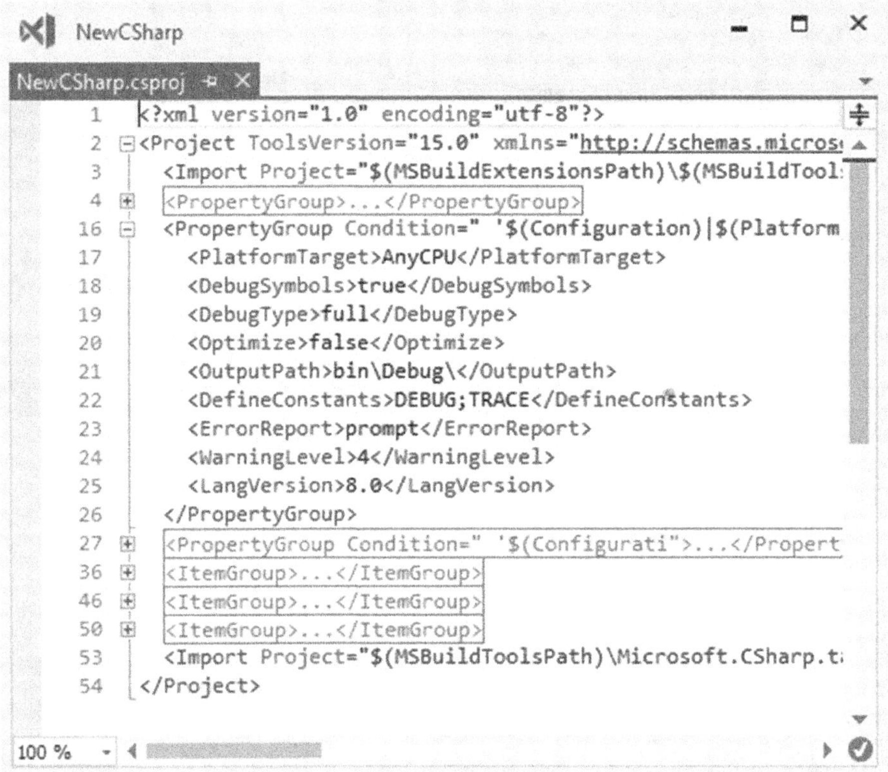

Figure 3-4. *Enable nullable reference types for project*

Then you need to add <NullableReferenceTypes>true</NullableReferenceTypes> just after the LangVersion element as can be seen in Figure 3-4.

Recap

To recap, in C# 8.0 we now have nullable reference types and non-nullable reference types. These enable you to tell the compiler exactly what your intent is with reference type variables.

In order to enable nullable reference type variables in C# 8.0, you need to use a new pragma #nullable. The compiler will interpret your intent in one of two ways. These are as follows.

A Reference Type Variable Can't Be Null

If reference type variables are not supposed to be null, the compiler will enforce that rule to ensure that it is safe to use the variable without checking if it is null or not. This means that the variable must be initialized to a non-null value. The variable can therefore never be assigned a null value.

A Reference Type Might Be Null

When we declare a nullable reference type variable, we are telling the compiler that the possibility exists that the variable value could be null. The compiler will now enforce different rules to ensure that you have checked for a null reference. You can therefore initialize these variables with the default null.

Recursive Patterns

Recursive patterns are a welcome addition to C#. You will remember that in C# 7, we saw the introduction of pattern matching. C# 8.0 takes this a step further by allowing patterns to contain other patterns. Consider the following class.

Listing 3-1. Person class

```
public class Person
{
    public int Age { get; }
    public string Name { get; }
    public bool RegisteredToVote { get; set; }

    public Person(string name, int age, bool registered)
    {
        Name = name;
        Age = age;
        RegisteredToVote = registered;
    }
}
```

The class contains a Boolean to indicate if the person is registered to vote. Recursive patterns will allow us to extract those persons that have not registered to vote by doing the following.

Listing 3-2. Recursive pattern

```
foreach (var person in personList)
{
    if (person is Person { RegisteredToVote: false })
    {
        WriteLine($"{person.Name} has not registered.");
    }
}
```

What we are saying here is that if an object in a list is of type Person and if that person has the RegisteredToVote property set to false, display the name of the person.

```
foreach (var person in personList)
{
    if (person is Person { RegisteredToVote: false, | })
    {
        WriteLine($"{person.Name} has not registered      Age:
    }                                                      Name:
}
```

Figure 3-5. *IntelliSense available*

You will also notice that Intellisense is available (Figure 3-5) if you need to add another condition to the pattern. Add the following eligibility property to your class.

Listing 3-3. Person class with eligibility property

```
public class Person
{
    public int Age { get; }
    public string Name { get; }
    public bool RegisteredToVote { get; set; }
    public bool EligibleToVote { get => Age > 18; }

    public Person(string name, int age, bool registered)
```

```
    {
        Name = name;
        Age = age;
        RegisteredToVote = registered;
    }
}
```

We can now check to see if a person is not registered to vote, but only return those people that are eligible to vote by doing the following.

Listing 3-4. Returning only eligible people not registered

```
foreach (var person in personList)
{
    if (person is Person { RegisteredToVote: false, EligibleToVote: true })
    {
        WriteLine($"{person.Name} has not registered.");
    }
}
```

Recursive patterns allow you to be more flexible and allow for more expressive code.

Ranges and Indices

Ranges and indices were designed in the first few months of 2018. What C# 8.0 allows us to do with indexed data structures is grab a slice of the array, string, or span.

Listing 3-5. An array of names

```
string[] names = { "Dirk", "Jane", "James", "Albert", "Sally" };
foreach (var name in names)
{
    // do something
}
```

Considering a standard array of names, we can iterate over the array in a foreach as in the previous code listing. With C# 8.0, however, we can now easily pull out only a part of the array as follows.

Listing 3-6. Pulling out a part of the array

```
string[] names = { "Dirk", "Jane", "James", "Albert", "Sally" };
foreach (var name in names[1..4])
{
    // do something
}
```

This allows us to iterate over a portion of the names in the array. The 1..4 is actually a range expression.

Please note that the endpoint of 4 in the preceding example is exclusive, which means that the element 4 is not included in [1..4].

C# has adopted a C-style approach to arrays, so the endpoint being exclusive is consistent with that approach. This means that in [1..4], the length of the slice we want is 4-1 = 3.

Another point to take note of is that the range expression does not have to form part of the indexing operation. It can be pulled out into its own variable with its own type called Range. This will allow the following code to be valid.

Listing 3-7. Using the Range type

```
string[] names = { "Dirk", "Jane", "James", "Albert", "Sally" };
Range range = 1..4;
foreach (var name in names[range])
{
    // do something
}
```

In the preceding code example, the range expression was an integer 1..4. In reality, they don't have to be. In actual fact, they're of a type called Index. The non-negative integer values convert to Index.

Because the range expression is of type Index, you can create an Index by using the new ^ operator.

Sometimes the new ^ operator is also referred to as the *hat* operator. Time will tell what is going to stick when referring to the ^ operator.

The new ^ operator means *from-end*, and so 1..^1 means 1 from the end. You can therefore have the following.

Listing 3-8. Using the "from-end" operator

```
string[] names = { "Dirk", "Jane", "James", "Albert", "Sally" };
foreach (var name in names[1..^1])
{
    // do something
}
```

The ^1 essentially cuts off an element at the end of the array, returning an array with the middle elements.

- Jane

- James

- Albert

There are some developers that argue that using ^ to mean *from-end* is confusing, especially since ^ means *from the beginning* in regex. But as Mads Torgersen (design lead for C#) commented, they decided to follow Python when working with *from-beginning* and *from-end* arithmetic.

Range expressions can be written in a few ways. These are explained as follows:

- The expression ..^1 is the same as 0..^1

- The expression 1.. is the same as 1..^0

- The expression .. is the same as 0..^0

The expression 0..^0 returns everything in the array (for example) from beginning to end. You can think of ^0 as the element right off the end.

Switch Expressions

In C# 7.0 we saw the inclusion of patterns in switch statements. You will remember that we had a look at pattern matching in Chapter 1. Consider the following class examples.

Listing 3-9. Class examples

```
public class Human : Species
{
    public string Name { get; }
    public bool RegisteredToVote { get; set; }
    public bool EligibleToVote { get => Age > 18; }

    public Human(string name, bool registered)
    {
        Name = name;
        RegisteredToVote = registered;
    }
}

public class Mammal : Species
{
    public string Name { get; }
    public Mammal(string name)
    {
        Name = name;
    }
}

public class Reptile : Species
{
    public string Name { get; }
    public bool LaysEggs { get; }
    public Reptile(string name, bool laysEggs)
    {
        Name = name;
        LaysEggs = laysEggs;
    }
}
```

```
}

public class Species
{
    public int Age { get; set; }
}
```

The classes are really basic and if we wanted to use pattern matching in a switch statement, we would typically do the following.

Listing 3-10. C# 7.0 switch statement

```
Species species = new Reptile("Snake", true);
species.Age = 2;

switch (species)
{
    case Human h:
        WriteLine($"{h.Name} is a {nameof(Human)}");
        break;
    case Mammal m:
        WriteLine($"{m.Name} is a {nameof(Mammal)}");
        break;
    case Reptile r:
        WriteLine($"{r.Name} is a {nameof(Reptile)}");
        break;
    default:
        WriteLine("Species could not be determined");
        break;
}
```

This is a valid code, but becomes somewhat cumbersome to write. In C# 8.0 you will be able to rewrite the code in the previous listing as follows.

Listing 3-11. Switch expression

```
var result = species switch
{
    Human h => $"{h.Name} is a {nameof(Human)}",
```

```
    Mammal m => $"{m.Name} is a {nameof(Mammal)}",
    Reptile r => $"{r.Name} is a {nameof(Reptile)}",
    _ => "Species could not be determined"
};
```

```
WriteLine(result);
```

C# 8.0 introduces switch expressions where the cases are expressions. Think of it as a lightweight version of switch statements.

You will notice that the `default` case uses a discard _ variable. Discards were discussed in Chapter 1 of this book in case you need to recap.

You will notice that the `case` keyword and the : have been replaced by the lambda => arrow. Another thing to note is that the body is now an expression and the selected body becomes the switch expression's result.

Should I Use Switch Expressions?

Personally, I find the switch expressions much nicer to read and write, especially when formatted as in Figure 3-6. The results of more focused and succinct code are evident in the fact that we reduced a 15-line case statement to only 7 lines of code.

```
var result = species switch
{
    Human h        => $"{h.Name} is a {nameof(Human)}",
    Mammal m       => $"{m.Name} is a {nameof(Mammal)}",
    Reptile r      => $"{r.Name} is a {nameof(Reptile)}",
    _              => "Species could not be determined"
};
```

Figure 3-6. *More readable code*

If you want to write switches using less code and that is more expressive, consider using switch expressions.

Property Patterns

Let us expand on our switch expression to differentiate between reptiles that lay eggs and reptiles that give birth to live young.

Yes, you get viviparous snakes that give birth to live young, e.g., green anacondas and boa constrictors.

Include a case in the `switch` statement that will check when a reptile has a property of `LayEggs` equal to `true` and output a different result based on that.

```
var result = species switch
{
    Human h                      => $"{h.Name} is a {nameof(Human)}",
    Mammal m                     => $"{m.Name} is a {nameof(Mammal)}",
    Reptile r when r.LaysEggs    => $"{r.Name} is a {nameof(Reptile)} that lays eggs",
    Reptile r                    => $"{r.Name} is a {nameof(Reptile)}",
    _                            => "Species could not be determined"
};
```

Figure 3-7. *Checking for viviparous reptiles*

C# 8.0 will now allow the pattern to dig deeper into the value that is being pattern matched. This means that you as a developer can make it a property pattern by adding curly braces to apply to the value's properties or fields. You can therefore rewrite the switch expression in Figure 3-7 as follows.

```
var result = species switch
{
    Human h                      => $"{h.Name} is a {nameof(Human)}",
    Mammal m                     => $"{m.Name} is a {nameof(Mammal)}",
    Reptile {LaysEggs: true } r  => $"{r.Name} is a {nameof(Reptile)} that lays eggs",
    Reptile r                    => $"{r.Name} is a {nameof(Reptile)}",
    _                            => "Species could not be determined"
};
```

Figure 3-8. *Switch expression with property pattern*

C# 8.0 also allows more optional elements with type patterns. If we are dealing with a `Reptile` that lays eggs, then we want its age. Here we can apply the `var` pattern to the `Age` property.

```
var result = species switch
{
    Human h                         => $"{h.Name} is a {nameof(Human)}",
    Mammal m                        => $"{m.Name} is a {nameof(Mammal)}",
    Reptile { LaysEggs: true } r    => $"{r.Name} is a {nameof(Reptile)} that lays eggs",
    Reptile { Age: var age }        => $"This {nameof(Reptile)} is {age} years old",
    _                               => "Species could not be determined"
};
```

Figure 3-9. *Omitting Reptile r*

Remember that var will always succeed and declares a new variable to hold the value (Figure 3-9). Therefore, the variable age gets to contain the value of r.Age, and we can drop r because it is never used (Figure 3-10).

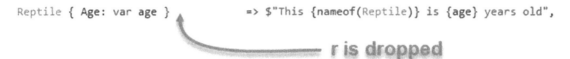

```
Reptile { Age: var age }        => $"This {nameof(Reptile)} is {age} years old",
```

r is dropped

Figure 3-10. *r can be dropped because it isn't used*

All patterns including property patterns require the value to be non-null. Replacing the fallback case with {} and null will deal with non-null patterns and nulls (Figure 3-11).

```
var result = species switch
{
    Human h                         => $"{h.Name} is a {nameof(Human)}",
    Mammal m                        => $"{m.Name} is a {nameof(Mammal)}",
    Reptile { LaysEggs: true } r    => $"{r.Name} is a {nameof(Reptile)} that lays eggs",
    Reptile { Age: var age }        => $"This {nameof(Reptile)} is {age} years old",
    { }                             => species.ToString(),
    null                            => "null"
};
```

Figure 3-11. *Cater for non-null objects and null*

An empty property pattern is dealt with by {} and null will catch all the nulls.

Target-Typed New Expressions

Microsoft has come a very long way from where they were to embracing the developer community. The thought process surrounding developers and what they can mean to the developer community at large is perfectly showcased in the following feature being introduced in C# 8.0.

This feature's implementation was in fact contributed by Alireza Habibi, a member of the community.

In the past, you would need to add the type when creating an array of Point, for example.

Listing 3-12. Point array before C# 8.0

```
Point[] ps = { new Point(1, 4), new Point(3, 2), new Point(9, 5) };
```

With C# 8.0, you can now simply change the code in the previous listing to be as follows.

Listing 3-13. Point array in C# 8.0

```
Point[] ps = { new (1, 4), new (3, 2), new (9, 5) };
```

The type is already given from the context. Therefore, in these situations, C# will allow you to omit the type.

Async Streams

Let us think back to async as discussed in Chapter 2. Asynchronous programming will allow you to write code that can perform long running tasks while still keeping your application responsive.

The basic idea is that we have these things called Tasks in .NET which represent a promise as it were of some future result. We might have an async method as follows.

Listing 3-14. Async method

```
static async Task Main(string[] args)
{
    var result = await GetSomethingAsync();

    WriteLine(result);
    ReadLine();
}

static async Task<int> GetSomethingAsync()
{
```

```
    await Task.Delay(1000);
    return 0;
}
```

You will notice that I am creating the Main method with the async modifier.

Async Main was introduced in C# 7.1 that now allows you to create the entry point for your application with the `async` modifier. If your program returns an exit code, you can declare a Main method that returns a `Task<int>` instead.

What is important to note here is the `await` operator. This allows you to insert a suspension point in the execution of the code until the awaited task finishes what it is busy with. This task therefore represents some ongoing work, and `await` can only be used when the method is modified with the async keyword.

We call such a method (that uses the `async` modifier) that contains one or several `await` expressions an *async method*. The code in the previous listing works fine for single results, but what about a continuous stream of results?

Think of a database that is queried for data which it can't return all at once. So, it needs to stream it, and the data will arrive at the calling code at certain intervals. Your code, however, wants to process this data in its own time. It is for this reason that C# 8.0 introduced IAsyncEnumerable<T> which is an asynchronous version of IEnumerable<T>. With this, you can essentially write the following code.

Listing 3-15. IAsyncEnumerable<T>

```
static IAsyncEnumerable<int> GetLotsAsync()
{
    await foreach(var item in GetSomethingAsync())
    {
        if (item > 8)
            yield return item;
    }
}
```

The code does an ordinary `await`, but you are able to use the usual language constructs (for example, the `foreach`) to consume the data.

When `yield return` is reached inside an iterator method, `expression` is returned and retains the current location in the code. If this code is run again, the code execution is restarted from that location the next time the iterator is called. To end the iteration, call `yield break` instead.

Think of this as an `async` iterator that combines `async` methods and iterator methods that allows you to use `await` and `yield return` inside of it.

OBSERVABLES VS. ASYNC STREAMS

During an interview with Mads Torgersen, a remark was made that async streams feel similar to observables or reactive extensions. Mads Torgersen explained that async streams are basically a pull model where you as the developer ask for something and then get it. Observables on the other hand use a push model when they have data.

With observables, the producer decides the timing of the data being delivered to the consumer. In async streams the consumer decides when it's ready to receive the data.

Using Declarations

Another nice addition to C# 8.0 is the feature of simplifying using statements. Traditionally, using statements introduce a level of nesting. Personally, I liked it, because it always felt like the using statement clearly shows when the resource is going to be cleaned up. This happens when the code execution moves past the closing curly brace.

Nevertheless, for simple cases, we now have using declarations in C# 8.0. Consider the following code listing that has a using statement when working with a SQL connection.

Listing 3-16. using statement pre-C# 8.0

```
string tsql = "[SQL QRY]";
string sqlConnStr = "[SQL Connection String]";
using (var con = new SqlConnection(sqlConnStr))
{
```

```
    SqlCommand cmd = new SqlCommand(tsql, con);
    //..
}
```

The `using` statement will clean up the connection etc. as soon as the code execution moves out of the using block. With C# 8.0, however, we can do the following.

Listing 3-17. Using declaration in C# 8.0

```
string tsql = "[SQL QRY]";
string sqlConnStr = "[SQL Connection String]";
using var con = new SqlConnection(sqlConnStr);
SqlCommand cmd = new SqlCommand(tsql, con);
```

`using` declarations are just local variable declarations. The only difference is that it now has a `using` keyword in front. The contents are therefore disposed of at the end of the current statement block.

Wrapping Up

The language features introduced in C# 8.0 are really exciting. I am sure that the C# team will be refining these and adding more as time goes by. Another exciting development is the speed at which point releases happen in C#. This is evident in the point releases we saw in C# 7. It is a good idea to keep up to date with these releases, just in case they decide to sneak in something really cool.

We had a look at nullable reference types that are now available, which allow you to use `string?` to indicate nullability on a string, for example. We then took a look at recursive patterns that allows patterns to contain other patterns. Ranges and indices were discussed next, which allow you to grab a slice of an array, string, or span. I then showed you how switch expressions work that can be seen as lightweight switch statements. Target-typed new expressions allowed you to omit the type when creating a `Point` array, because the type is given from the context. Async streams were then discussed and allow you to use an asynchronous version of `IEnumerable` called `IAsyncEnumerable`. Lastly, we had a look at using declarations that simplify using statements by not introducing a level of nesting.

In the next chapter, we will have a look at how to create responsive web applications using ASP.NET MVC, Bootstrap, jQuery, and SCSS.

CHAPTER 4

Responsive Web Applications Using ASP.NET MVC

Responsive web applications are essential in modern application development. Users need to be able to view the content of your web application on any device. This means that a web application needs to resize itself based on whatever device it is being viewed on.

In this chapter you will create a simple task management system that uses the Bootstrap code framework to remain responsive. We will have a look at the following:

- Creating your ASP.NET MVC application

- Referencing jQuery and Bootstrap

- Setting up and using SCSS

- Creating models, controllers, views, and using Razor

- Adding a plugin

- Testing your responsive layout using Chrome

- Debugging your jQuery using Chrome Developer Tools

I will be using the latest version of Visual Studio 2019 that was available at the time of writing this chapter.

© Dirk Strauss 2019
D. Strauss, *Exploring Advanced Features in C#*, https://doi.org/10.1007/978-1-4842-4856-0_4

Creating Your ASP.NET MVC Application

The new start window in Visual Studio 2019 does look quite a bit different. You will notice that it now has five main sections. These are

- Open recent

- Clone or checkout code

- Open a project or solution

- Open a local folder

- Create a new project

Having your recent projects to the left that are pinned or unpinned is quite handy, and this should tell you something about the new start window.

I will be going into more depth on this and other new features in Visual Studio 2019 in a later chapter, so keep an eye out for that.

The goal that the Visual Studio team had with the new start window was to give you quick access to the most common ways you would access your code. For most it would be cloning from a repository or opening an existing project as seen in Figure 4-1.

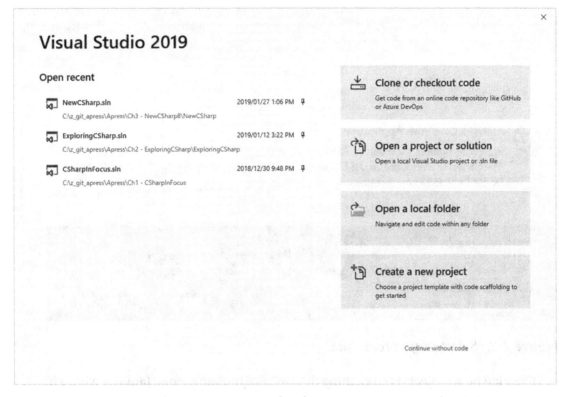

Figure 4-1. *Visual Studio 2019 New Project screen*

For now, you will be creating a new project, so click that option to get going.

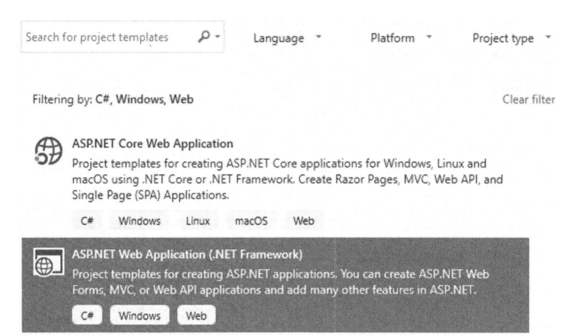

Figure 4-2. *Select project template*

Creating new projects is something that you are probably quite familiar with. The new project dialog (as seen in Figure 4-2) has been cleaned up a bit and no longer includes a table of contents style of nodes and sub-nodes.

It now includes a *Recent project templates* section that is similar to the *Open recent* in the start window. For this project, we will be selecting an ASP.NET Web Application using the .NET Framework.

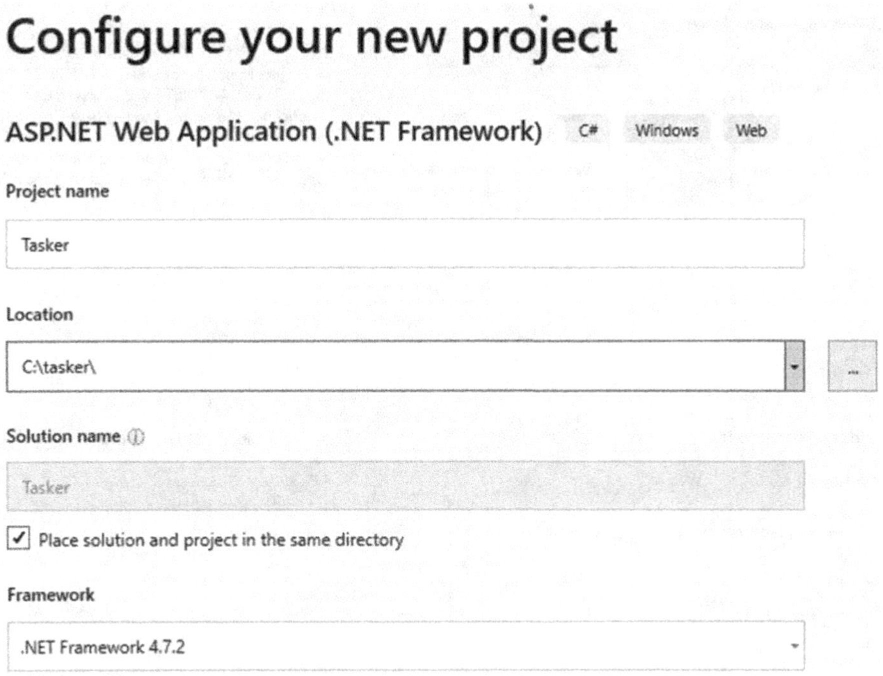

Configure your new project

ASP.NET Web Application (.NET Framework)   C#   Windows   Web

Project name

Tasker

Location

C:\tasker\

Solution name ⓘ

Tasker

☑ Place solution and project in the same directory

Framework

.NET Framework 4.7.2

Figure 4-3. *Configuring your project*

After selecting the project template, you are allowed to configure your new project
(Figure 4-3). We are going to create a simple task management application that will
manage tasks and color code them according to some state we will be defining later on.
Also note that you can select the .NET Framework version in the last combo menu.

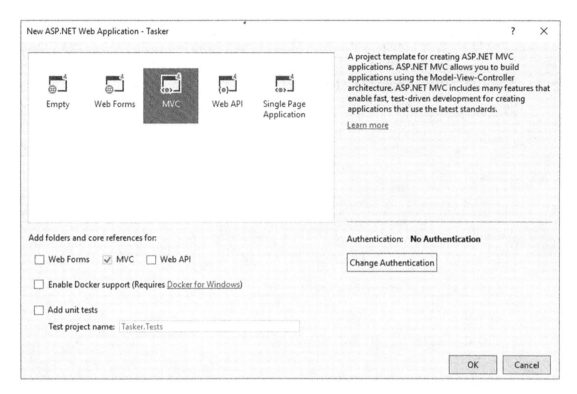

Figure 4-4. *Selecting an MVC project*

Next you will see the familiar project configuration screen where you can select the type of web application you want to create (Figure 4-4). Select MVC here and don't worry about enabling Docker support or adding unit tests. We also don't require any authentication in this project.

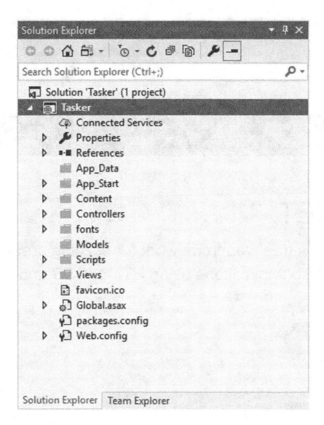

Figure 4-5. *The created project in Solution Explorer*

Visual Studio now goes ahead and creates your ASP.NET MVC application with all the default boilerplate code. After it is finished, you should see the Solution Explorer with the following project as in Figure 4-5. If you see this, then you are ready to start creating your application.

Build your project and press *F5* to run your project.

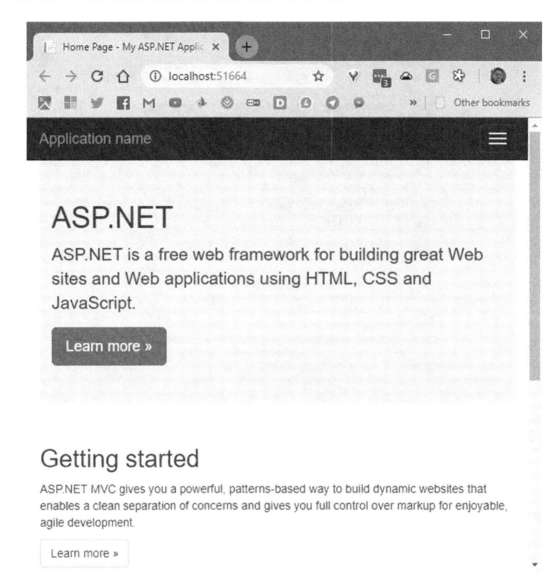

Figure 4-6. *Running your ASP.NET MVC application*

If everything is set up correctly, you will see the default web application start up in your browser.

Referencing jQuery and Bootstrap

In your *Solution Explorer*, if you expand the *App_Start* folder, you will see a class called BundleConfig. It is here that you will see references to CSS and JavaScript files.

Bundling and minification improve request load time. They do this by reducing the number of requests to the server, and in doing so reduce the size of the requested assets.

You will notice that the `RegisterBundles` method contains references to the jQuery and Bootstrap files stored in the Scripts folder. It also includes the stylesheets contained in the Content folder.

Listing 4-1. The BundleConfig class

```
public static void RegisterBundles(BundleCollection bundles)
{
    bundles.Add(new ScriptBundle("~/bundles/jquery")
        .Include("~/Scripts/jquery-{version}.js"));

    bundles.Add(new ScriptBundle("~/bundles/jqueryval")
        .Include("~/Scripts/jquery.validate*"));

    // Use the development version of Modernizr to develop
    // with and learn from. Then, when you're ready for
    // production, use the build tool at
    // https://modernizr.com to pick only the tests you need.
    bundles.Add(new ScriptBundle("~/bundles/modernizr")
        .Include("~/Scripts/modernizr-*"));

    bundles.Add(new ScriptBundle("~/bundles/bootstrap")
        .Include("~/Scripts/bootstrap.js"));

    bundles.Add(new StyleBundle("~/Content/css")
        .Include("~/Content/bootstrap.css",
            "~/Content/site.css"));
}
```

You will notice that we have a `ScriptBundle` for js files and a `StyleBundle` for our css files. It is here in the `ScriptBundle` that we will be adding another reference to the *jquery-ui.min.js* file.

jQuery UI is a collection of UI controls, assets, widgets, and themes that are built on top of the jQuery JavaScript library. Use this if you need to include some form of user interaction.

In your browser, go to `http://jqueryui.com/download/` and make your selections in the *Core, Interactions, Widgets,* and *Effects* categories.

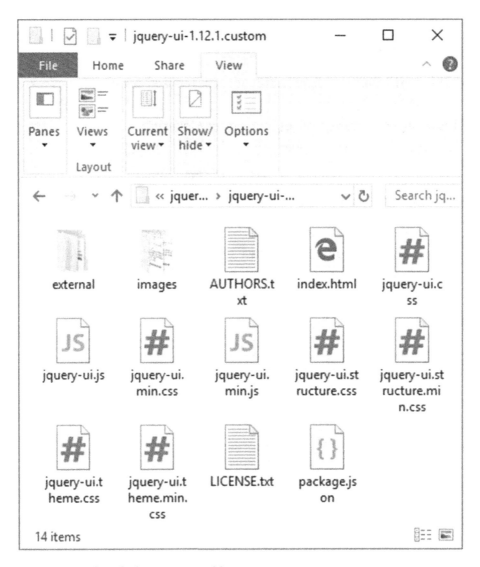

Figure 4-7. *Downloaded jQuery UI files*

I want to allow the user to drag elements (the task items in particular) around on the web page. I therefore only need to include the draggable interaction, but I will go ahead and include everything in case I need to use other interactions later on.

The two files I am interested in are *jquery-ui.js* and *jquery-ui.min.js.* Add these two files to your *Scripts* folder of your project.

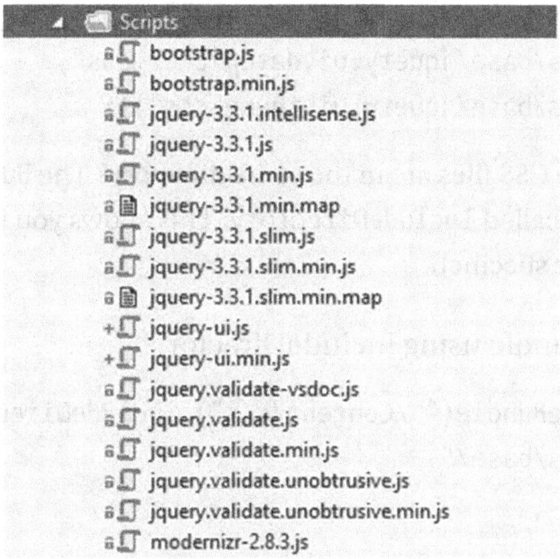

Figure 4-8. Adding the jQuery UI files

After you have added the files, you need to update your `RegisterBundles` method in the `BundleConfig` class by adding an `Include` with the path to the minified file.

Listing 4-2. Modified RegisterBundles method

```
bundles.Add(new ScriptBundle("~/bundles/jquery")
    .Include("~/Scripts/jquery-{version}.js")
    .Include("~/Scripts/jquery-ui.min.js"));
```

This will now create a bundle named `~/bundles/jquery` and it will include all the appropriate files you specify as well as the files matching the wild card `{version}` string.

Creating Bundles

We can create bundles by specifying an array of strings in the `Include` method. Each string is the virtual path to a resource. Here is an example of a StyleBundle specifying the virtual paths to several CSS files.

135

Listing 4-3. A StyleBundle

```
bundles.Add(new StyleBundle("~/Content/css").Include(
    "~/Content/themes/base/jquery.ui.code.css",
    "~/Content/themes/base/jquery.ui.button.css",
    "~/Content/themes/base/jquery.ui.slider.css",
    "~/Content/themes/base/jquery.ui.tabs.css",
    "~/Content/themes/base/jquery.ui.datepicker.css",
    "~/Content/themes/base/jquery.ui.theme.css"));
```

Notice how all these CSS files are in the same directory? The Bundle class also provides a method called IncludeDirectory. This allows you to modify your StyleBundle to be more succinct.

Listing 4-4. A StyleBundle using IncludeDirectory

```
bundles.Add(new StyleBundle("~/Content/css").IncludeDirectory(
    "~/Content/themes/base/"
    , "*.css"
    ,false));
```

I have specified a virtual directory path and also specified a search pattern to match only the CSS files. The last parameter set to false specifies that subdirectories be excluded from the search.

Referencing Bundles in Views

We are going to be having a closer look at Views in a next section of this chapter. I need to however mention here that bundles are referenced in a view using the Render method. For CSS we use Styles.Render and for JavaScript we use Scripts.Render. Have a look in the shared *_Layout.cshtml* view to see how the stylesheets and scripts are rendered. The *_Layout.cshtml* view is shared among all other views (think of it as a master page in old ASP.NET). These scripts and stylesheets referenced here are therefore included on all pages for the site.

Setting Up and Using SCSS

Now that I have referenced the jQuery UI file, I want to create a custom stylesheet for my application. For this I will create a .scss stylesheet. Create a folder called *scss* in your project and add a new SCSS file called *customstyles.scss* to that folder.

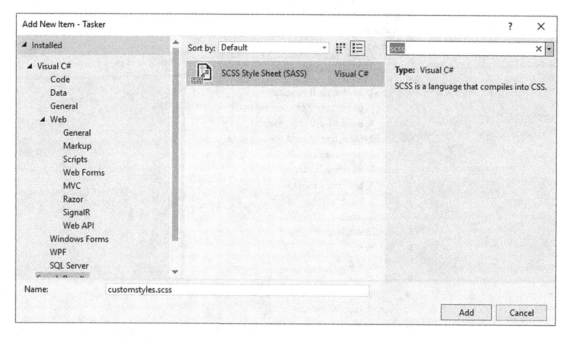

Figure 4-9. *Add new SCSS stylesheet*

When you have added the folder and file to your project, your solution should look as in the next image.

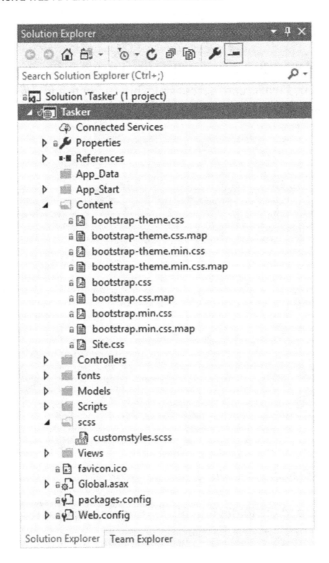

Figure 4-10. *Added scss folder and customstyles file*

You will notice that the *Content* folder contains our CSS files. This is logically where we want to place our *customstyles.css* file. This CSS file will be generated from our scss file created under the *scss* folder. To do this, we need to install a tool called *Web Compiler* created by Mads Kristensen. Head on over to the *Extensions* menu in Visual Studio 2019 and click *Extensions and Updates.*

Figure 4-11. *Extensions and Updates*

After you download the tool, Visual Studio 2019 will schedule the installation of Web Compiler.

You need to close Visual Studio down before the installation of Web Compiler starts.

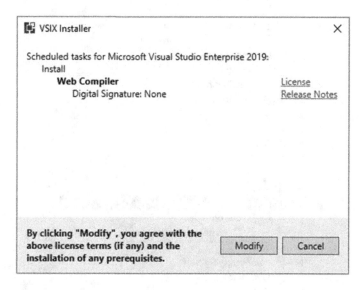

Figure 4-12. *Web Compiler installation*

After Web Compiler is installed, start Visual Studio 2019. Have a look at the customstyles.scss file we created earlier. It just contains the following code.

Listing 4-5. Contents of customstyles.scss file

```
body {
}
```

We will be adding some styling code to this file in a moment, but first right-click the file and click *Web Compiler* ➤ *Compile file* or hold down *Shift+Alt+Q* to compile the file into CSS.

The Web Compiler we installed earlier jumps into action and creates CSS files called *customstyles.css* and *customstyles.min.css* for us. There is only one problem, the generated CSS files are not in the correct folder. We want the generated CSS files in the Content folder of our project.

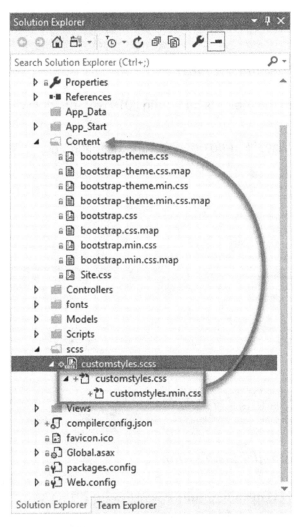

Figure 4-13. *Generated CSS files*

This is easily fixed. When the Web Compiler generated the CSS files, it also created a file called *compilerconfig.json* for you in the project root. Go ahead and open the *compilerconfig.json* file.

Listing 4-6. Compiler configuration for the scss file

```
[
  {
    "outputFile": "scss/customstyles.css",
    "inputFile": "scss/customstyles.scss"
  }
]
```

You will notice that the file contains a setting for the output path for the generated CSS file. The path is the same as the input file path. Modify your outputFile path as in the next code listing.

Listing 4-7. Modified Compiler configuration for the scss file

```
[
  {
    "outputFile": "Content/customstyles.css",
    "inputFile": "scss/customstyles.scss"
  }
]
```

When you save the *compilerconfig.json* file, another compilation is automatically done.

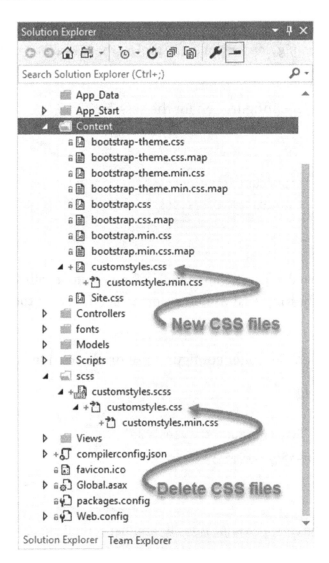

Figure 4-14. *Generated CSS files*

This creates the CSS files in the correct *Content* folder. You can go ahead and delete the CSS files under the *scss* folder. These will never be updated when we modify our scss file.

What Exactly Is SCSS?

SCSS is an implementation of SASS (Syntactically Awesome Style Sheets). In fact, SASS supports two types of syntax, namely, SCSS and SASS. The main difference between SCSS and SASS is the use of curly braces and semicolons that SCSS uses. Being used to C#, it makes more sense to use SCSS.

SCSS is fully compliant with CSS, so all your existing code will still work. The benefits of SCSS are

- Being able to use variables

- Allows nested syntax

- Allows the use of mixins

- Allows the use of partials to modularize code

- Being able to use @extend to inherit and extend classes

- Allows the use of functions

This allows you to split up the code to style your application and separate concerns regarding specific styling in your application. Go ahead and add another scss file called *_variables.scss* to your *scss* folder. Take note that you must include the underscore before the filename to mark this as a partial scss file.

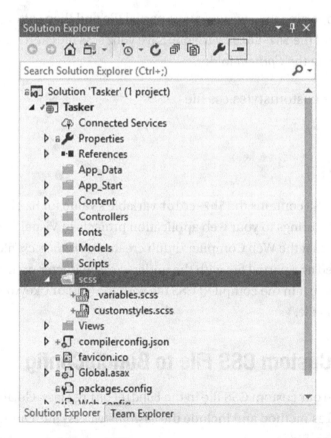

Figure 4-15. *The _variables.scss file*

Add the following code to the _variables.scss file.

Listing 4-8. The color variable for H2 tags

```
/* Header Colors */
$h2-color: #9DB941;
```

This is just a variable (denoted by a $ sign) that sets a value for the H2 elements in your markup. Next, modify your *customstyles.scss* file as follows.

Listing 4-9. Custom styling for H2 elements

```
@import "_variables.scss";

h2{
    color: $h2-color;
}
```

Here we are importing the *_variables.scss* partial file and then setting H2 element colors to the value of the $h2-color variable. Save your scss files and have a look at the *customstyles.css* file in the *Content* folder.

Listing 4-10. The customstyles.css file

```
/* Header Colors */
h2 {
  color: #9DB941; }
```

The compiled CSS contains the $h2-color variable's value for H2 elements. This is the power that SCSS brings to your web application projects in Visual Studio.

You will notice that the Web Compiler didn't create a *variables.css* file. This is because it is marked as a partial file with the underscore character prefixing the file name. We include it in the compiled CSS file with the @import keyword in the customstyles.scss file.

Adding Our Custom CSS File to BundleConfig

We need to include our custom CSS file in the BundleConfig class. Go ahead and edit the RegisterBundles method and include the *customstyles.css* file. Our method currently references the *site.css* file.

Listing 4-11. StyleBundle referencing site.css

```
bundles.Add(new StyleBundle("~/Content/css")
            .Include("~/Content/bootstrap.css",
                "~/Content/site.css"));
```

Change this to reference our custom CSS file by removing the *site.css* reference and adding our *customstyles.css* reference instead.

Listing 4-12. StyleBundle referencing customstyles.css

```
bundles.Add(new StyleBundle("~/Content/css")
            .Include("~/Content/bootstrap.css",
                "~/Content/customstyles.css"));
```

We have now successfully referenced the stylesheet that we will be using throughout our application to style the elements as needed.

Creating Models, Controllers, Views and Using Razor

Before we can go and create views, we first need to create a model and a controller for our Task application. The whole premise of MVC is to separate concerns based on the role of each part of your application. As you probably know, MVC stands for *M*odel, *V*iew, and *C*ontroller. Let's recap the responsibility of each section of MVC.

What Is a Controller?

When the user makes a request to the browser, the controller determines what response is sent back to the user. It is responsible for controlling the flow of logic within the ASP. NET MVC application. You will notice that our application contained a *HomeController* by default. It is merely a C# class that initially contains a few methods called Index, About, and Contact. If you had to enter the URL *Home/Index*, then the controller would invoke the Index method. It is here that you would add additional methods (or actions) to match your views.

What Is a View?

If you have a look at the *HomeController*, you will notice that the methods each return a View. Expanding the *Views* folder in your *Solution Explorer*, you will notice that it contains a *Home* folder with three views that match the methods in the *HomeController* class. The *HomeController* therefore will look for a view called *Index* when the Index method is requested by the URL *Home/Index*. It is therefore important that you create your views in the correct place. Calling *Home/Index* will look for the *Index* view located at *Views\Home\Index.cshtml*. These views contain the markup for your web page.

What Is a Model?

A model is also just a C# class that contains all of the application's business logic, any validation needed, as well as all the database logic. Using Entity Framework as a database, for example, will have its logic contained in the Models folder. This means that your View must only contain the code needed to display the data in the web page. Your controller must only contain the minimum amount of code in order to select the correct view and redirect the user to other actions. The model should contain the rest of the code logic. A general rule of thumb is that if your controller is getting too complex or contains a lot of code, then you need to consider moving that logic out to a model. In most situations you should strive for skinny controllers and fat models.

What Is Routing?

Those of you that come from ASP.NET will remember that creating an ASP.NET web page meant that you needed a one-to-one match between the URL the user typed in and the page that was being requested. What I mean by this is that if the user requested a page called *DisplayTasks.aspx*, that page had to exist.

In ASP.NET MVC, this is not true. The URL that the user types in does not correspond to the files in your application. With MVC the URL that the user enters is matched up with an action (one of those methods mentioned earlier) in the controller. In the *HomeController* of our application, we have the actions *Index*, *About*, and *Contact*.

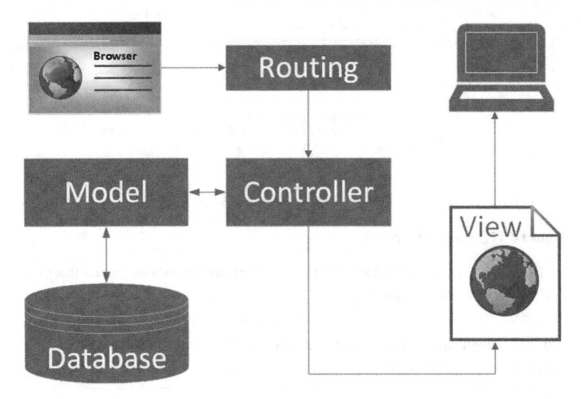

Figure 4-16. *The MVC design pattern*

This mapping of browser requests to controller actions is what is called routing in ASP.NET MVC. Incoming requests are routed to controller actions. This means that if the user requests *Home/Contact*, then the *Contact* action on the *HomeController* will be run. This also doesn't mean that the *Contact* view is returned. Remember we said that the job of the controller is to decide the flow of logic in the application? You could have different contact views, and the controller will make the decision of which view to return based on some logic (country of origin, for example). If the country of origin is one where the native language is not English, then the controller can return a different view with different contact details and in a different language.

How Routing Works

The incoming requests are handled by ASP.NET via a routing table that is created when your app starts for the first time. You can see this in the *Global.asax.cs* file in the root of the project.

```
0 references | Dirk Strauss, 7 days ago | 1 author, 1 change
public class MvcApplication : System.Web.HttpApplication
{
    0 references | Dirk Strauss, 7 days ago | 1 author, 1 change
    protected void Application_Start()
    {
        AreaRegistration.RegisterAllAreas();
        FilterConfig.RegisterGlobalFilters(GlobalFilters.Filters);
        RouteConfig.RegisterRoutes(RouteTable.Routes);
        BundleConfig.RegisterBundles(BundleTable.Bundles);
    }
}
```

Route table being created

Figure 4-17. *Route table creation*

It is created in a method called `Application_Start`, and you will also notice that this is where the bundles are registered too.

You will remember we said in a previous section that bundling and minification improve request load times.

If you have a look in the *RouteConfig.cs* file in the *App_Start* folder, you will see that our route table only consists of a single default route.

```
1 reference | Dirk Strauss, 7 days ago | 1 author, 1 change
public static void RegisterRoutes(RouteCollection routes)
{
    routes.IgnoreRoute("{resource}.axd/{*pathInfo}");

    routes.MapRoute(
        name: "Default",
        url: "{controller}/{action}/{id}",
        defaults: new
        {
            controller = "Home"
            , action = "Index"
            , id = UrlParameter.Optional
        } );
}
```

Figure 4-18. *RegisterRoutes method*

All incoming requests are broken up into three segments. You will notice that these segments are the sections between the forward slashes.

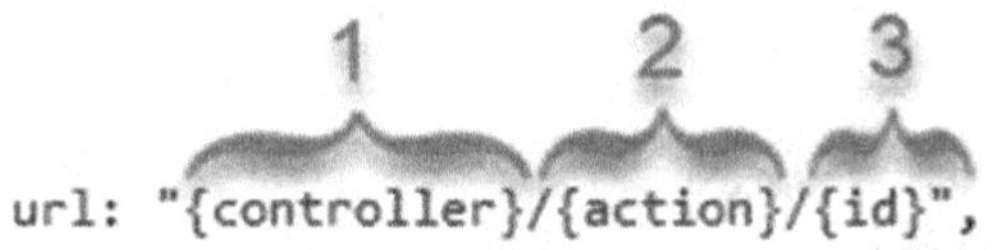

Figure 4-19. *Route segments*

The default route also gives your application the default values for the three segments. This means that, by default, when your application starts up, it will go to the default *Home/Index* route. The third section, the id, is marked as optional.

If you had to enter a URL in your browser of *Task/Display*, then based on the make up of your default route, you will need to have a controller called `TaskController` that contains an action (method) called `Display`. This, in a nutshell, is how routing works.

Creating Your Model

Let's start adding the meat of our Task application. We will start off by adding our model, then creating our controller, and lastly design our view. This will give us a workable application that we can expand to meet the needs of the design specification.

If you don't have a folder in your solution called *Models*, create one and create a class in that folder called *Task*.

Figure 4-20. *Creating the Task model*

When you have created your *Task* model, add the following code to your model.

Listing 4-13. The Task model code

```
public class Task
{
    public int TaskID { get; set; }
    public string TaskTitle { get; set; }
    public string TaskBody { get; set; }
    public DateTime DueDate { get; set; }
}
```

We will simulate the database query by stubbing our data in a method called
GetTasks that returns a List<Task> object. Add the following code to your Task model.

Listing 4-14. GetTasks method

```
public List<Task> GetTasks()
{
    return new List<Task>()
    {
        new Task ()
        {
            TaskID = 1
            , TaskTitle = "Review MVC tutorials"
            , TaskBody = "Make some time to view MVA videos"
            , DueDate = DateTime.Now
        },
        new Task ()
        {
            TaskID = 2
            , TaskTitle = "Create Test Project"
            , TaskBody = "Create a test project for demo at work"
            , DueDate = DateTime.Now.AddDays(1)
        },
        new Task ()
        {
            TaskID = 3
            , TaskTitle = "Lunch with Mary"
            , TaskBody = "Remember to make lunch reservations"
            , DueDate = DateTime.Now.AddDays(2)
        },
        new Task ()
        {
            TaskID = 4
            , TaskTitle = "Car Service"
            , TaskBody = "Have the car serviced before trip to HQ"
            , DueDate = DateTime.Now.AddDays(3)
        }
    };
}
```

For now, we will rely on this method to return our Task objects, as if they were read from a database. We now need to add the controller that will take care of our tasks. Let's do that next.

Creating Your Controller

If you expand the *Controllers* folder, you will see the default HomeController that was added for us when we created our application. It is in this *Controllers* folder that all our controllers will live. Right-click the folder and add a new controller for tasks. For now, just select to add an empty controller. Call the class TaskController, following the MVC convention for controllers, and click the *Add* button.

Listing 4-15. The default TaskController code

```
namespace Tasker.Controllers
{
    public class TaskController : Controller
    {
        // GET: Task
        public ActionResult Index()
        {
            return View();
        }
    }
}
```

The controller is created with the default code for the Index action. It doesn't really do much at this point, but is a nice scaffold from which you can work off of.

It is during this scaffolding process that we see something interesting happen. If you expand your *Views* folder, you will notice a new folder called *Task*.

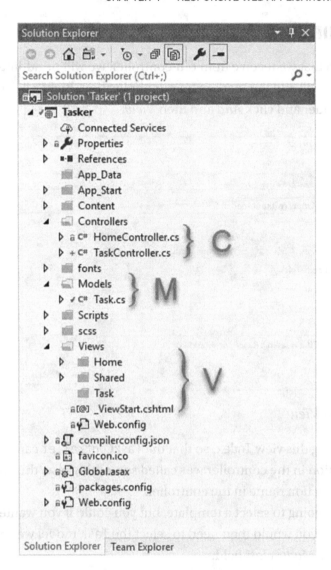

Figure 4-21. *The created Model, Views, and Controllers*

This is Visual Studio telling you that the views you create for your `TaskController` should live in the *Task* folder under *Views*. You will also notice the way MVC is structured, which in my opinion is a very logical one. The `TaskController` needs a little bit more code, which we will come back to. Right now, our application needs a view to display the data coming from our controller. Let's create one now.

Creating Your View

To display the data that we receive from our controller, we will be adding a view. It is to this view that we will add the markup for our application. Right-click the *Task* folder under the *Views* folder and click *Add* and then *View*.

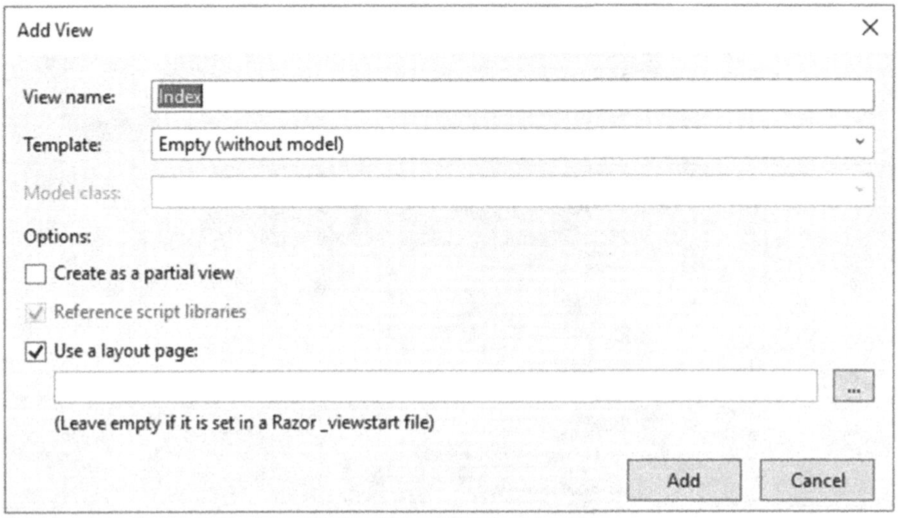

Figure 4-22. *Add View*

We will be calling this view Index, so that the TaskController can map correctly to this view. If the action in the controller was called something else, this view name would have to match that action name in the controller.

We are also not going to select a template, but you could if you wanted to. If you selected a template, you would then need to select the Task model we created earlier and enter that in the *Model class* field.

A very basic view is created with the following markup.

Listing 4-16. Basic view markup

```
@{
    ViewBag.Title = "Index";
}

<h2>Index</h2>
```

We need to expand this code slightly so that we can display our tasks in a logical way. We need to get a count of the tasks we have in our model. Modify your code as follows.

Listing 4-17. Modified multi-statement block

```
@model IEnumerable<Tasker.Models.Task>
@{
    ViewBag.Title = "Index";

    var iTaskCount = 0;
    iTaskCount = Model.Count();
}
```

You will notice that the first line indicates that our Index view is strongly typed to our Task class. The Razor view engine will now be able to understand that the Index view has been passed a Task object. The benefit of this is that we can now access all the properties of the model. More importantly, we can do this using Intellisense inside the markup of the web page.

The next thing we are going to do is write the HTML code for our view. It is here that you could be a bit more creative than I was. I had the idea of a Trello-type page where you can freely move task items between columns.

We will be creating three columns called *Pipeline*, *In progress*, and *Completed*. Our first column will contain the tasks and will look as follows.

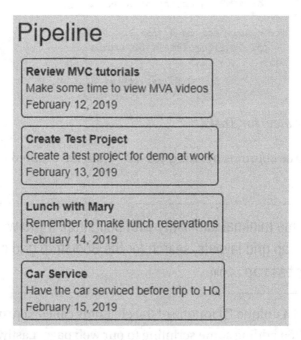

Figure 4-23. *The first task column*

As mentioned earlier, you can style the markup in any way you like. I opted to use a three-column layout, so this is what I did. Consider the following image.

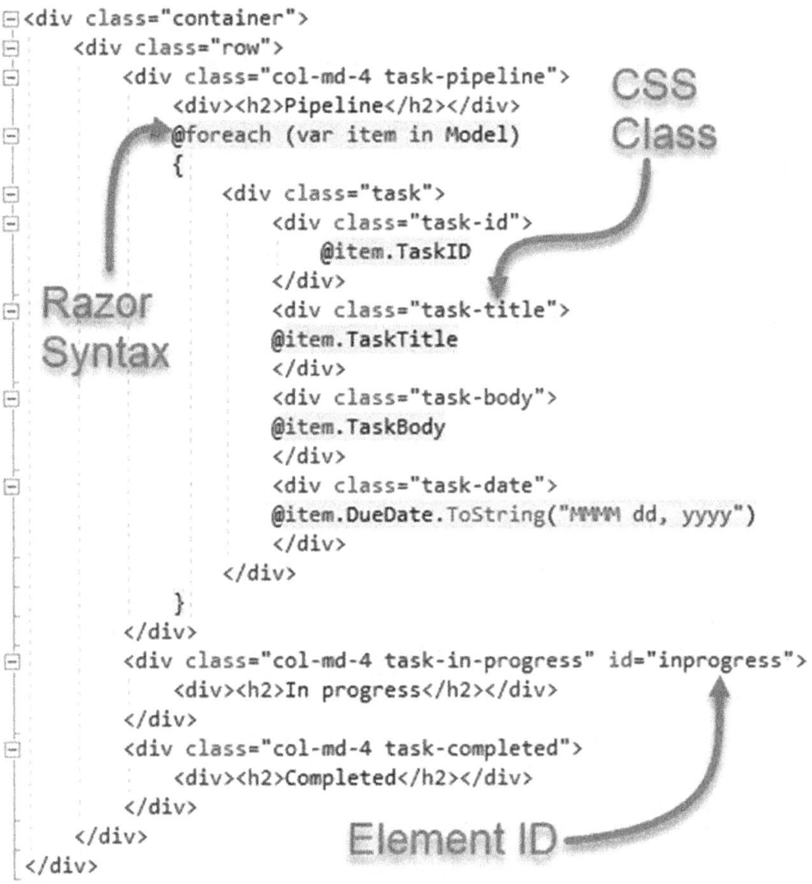

Figure 4-24. *Index view for Tasks*

I have created three columns by using `col-md-4` and have added Razor logic to the first column only.

I have assumed some minimal familiarity with Bootstrap. If you want to read more on the Bootstrap grid layouts, search for the Bootstrap grid examples on `https://getbootstrap.com`.

I have also added a unique ID for one of the elements called `inprogress`. We will need this later on when adding some scripting to our web page. Lastly, I have added Razor syntax. Let's expand a bit on what it is and how it works.

What Is Razor?

I want to pause here for a while and explain what Razor is. It is based on the C# language, but also supports Visual Basic. It is a programming syntax that allows you to embed server-based code in a web page. From the preceding image, you can see that we are left with a page that contains two types of content. These are client content and server code. The client content is all the markup that you are used to seeing in a web page. This is all the HTML elements, JavaScript, CSS, and plain text.

Our CSS is going to be extracted out into the SCSS file that will compile into our *customstyles* CSS stylesheet.

The server code is added in between the client content using Razor. The server code (as the name suggests) is run before the page is sent to the browser. This is really powerful, because it means that you can dynamically create client content based on conditions in the server code. Consider the following logic.

```
@model IEnumerable<Tasker.Models.Task>
@{
        ViewBag.Title = "Index";    Count Task Items

        var iTaskCount = 0;
        iTaskCount = Model.Count();
}
                  Dynamically create client content
@if (iTaskCount > 1)
    {
        <h2>You have @iTaskCount Tasks</h2>
    }
else if (iTaskCount > 0)
    {
        <h2>You only have @iTaskCount Task</h2>
    }
else
    {
        <h2>You have no Tasks</h2>
    }
```

Figure 4-25. *Use Razor to dynamically create client content*

Here you can see that we are dynamically creating the page heading, based on the number of tasks we have.

If your heading does not display, consider temporarily removing the `navbar` element defined in the _Layout.cshtml file located in the *Shared* folder of your project.

We store the task count in a variable called `iTaskCount`. This variable can easily be used in our page. We can mix it in between the HTML syntax and other Razor syntax. When the variable is used on its own, you must prefix the variable with the @ symbol.

How to Write Razor

The following is true for using Razor syntax in your web pages. When you want to add Razor code to your page, you need to use the @ character. The @ character can be used to start an inline expression, multi-statement block, or a single statement block.

Listing 4-18. Single statement block

```
@{ var iTotal = 3; }
```

This single statement block can be used anywhere in your web page's markup. Next, if you need to define an inline expression, you need to do the following.

Listing 4-19. Inline expression

```
<h2>You have @iTaskCount Tasks</h2>
```

This is really useful if you need to display variable values in your web page. In the code sample, it is used to display the number of tasks. Lastly, you can use multi-statement blocks.

Listing 4-20. Multi-statement block

```
@{
    ViewBag.Title = "Index";

    var iTaskCount = 0;
    iTaskCount = Model.Count();
}
```

This is the code we modified in Listing 4-17. If you need to include several code statements in your page, multi-statement blocks are the way to go.

Remember that inside the @{ } block, the code statements must still end with a semicolon. The only time that you do not have to include the semicolon is when you are adding an inline expression.

The power of Razor is that it allows you to use variables directly on your web page and mix the variable in between other HTML markup.

Linking Everything Together

Before we can run our Task application, we need to link the bits we have written together. We have created a model, a controller, and a view.

The complete Index view you have created needs to contain the following code.

Listing 4-21. The Index view code

```
@model IEnumerable<Tasker.Models.Task>
@{
    ViewBag.Title = "Index";

    var iTaskCount = 0;
    iTaskCount = Model.Count();
}

@if (iTaskCount > 1)
{
    <h2>You have @iTaskCount Tasks</h2>
}
else if (iTaskCount > 0)
{
    <h2>You only have @iTaskCount Task</h2>
}
else
{
    <h2>You have no Tasks</h2>
}

<div class="container">
    <div class="row">
        <div class="col-md-4 task-pipeline">
```

```
            <div><h2>Pipeline</h2></div>
            @foreach (var item in Model)
            {
                <div class="task">
                    <div class="task-id">
                        @item.TaskID
                    </div>
                    <div class="task-title">
                        @item.TaskTitle
                    </div>
                    <div class="task-body">
                        @item.TaskBody
                    </div>
                    <div class="task-date">
                        @item.DueDate.ToString("MMMM dd, yyyy")
                    </div>
                </div>
            }
        </div>
        <div class="col-md-4 task-in-progress" id="inprogress">
            <div><h2>In progress</h2></div>
        </div>
        <div class="col-md-4 task-completed">
            <div><h2>Completed</h2></div>
        </div>
    </div>
</div>
```

Let's swing back to our TaskController class and modify the code there to pass the Task model to our view.

Listing 4-22. Modified TaskController class

```
public class TaskController : Controller
{
    // GET: Task
    public ActionResult Index()
```

```
    {
        Task task = new Task();
        List<Task> tasks = task.GetTasks();
        return View(tasks);
    }
}
```

Next, I want to tell my application that when my application starts, the Index action of my TaskController needs to be run. This will display the Index view we have just completed. To do this, we need to change the default routing. Expand the *App_Start* folder in your solution.

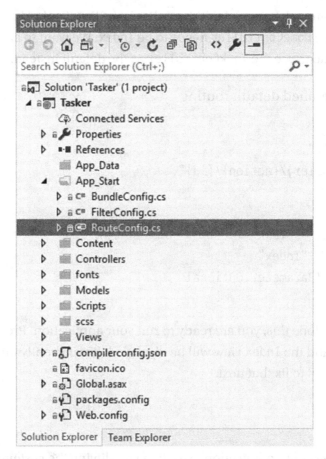

Figure 4-26. *RouteConfig class*

Here you will see the following code.

Listing 4-23. Default routing

```
routes.MapRoute(
    name: "Default",
    url: "{controller}/{action}/{id}",
    defaults: new
    {
        controller = "Home"
        , action = "Index"
        , id = UrlParameter.Optional
    });
```

Here we are stating that the default controller is the `HomeController` and that the default action in the `HomeController` needs to be `Index`. We want to change the default, so modify your code to use the `TaskController` as the default instead.

Listing 4-24. Modified default routing

```
routes.MapRoute(
    name: "Default",
    url: "{controller}/{action}/{id}",
    defaults: new
    {
        controller = "Task"
        , action = "Index"
        , id = UrlParameter.Optional
    });
```

After you have done this, you are ready to run your application. Pressing F5 will start your application, and the `Index` view will be displayed. It is currently unstyled and looks a bit ugly, so we need to fix that next.

Add Styling

To add some styling to our application, we will be modifying the *customstyles.scss* file we added earlier. You will recall that this file is compiled into the CSS file used in the application. Edit the customstyles.scss file and add the following code to it.

Listing 4-25. Custom styling

```css
.task {
    border: 1px solid blue;
    border-radius: 5px;
    padding: 5px;
    margin: 5px;

    .task-id {
        display: none;
    }

    .task-title {
        font-weight: bold;
    }
}

.task-pipeline, .task-in-progress, .task-completed {
    min-height: 500px;
}

.task-pipeline {
    background-color: powderblue;
}

.task-in-progress {
    background-color: thistle;
    z-index: -1;
}

.task-completed {
    background-color: plum;
    z-index: -1;
}
```

You will notice that these are the class names we added in the Index view for the Task item. Save this file to ensure it compiles and run your application again. This time, you will see that the styles are applied and that the page looks much better.

It is therefore logical that you should use this method of styling your application. As mentioned in a previous section, SCSS provides some really powerful features that you can use.

Add Some jQuery

In a previous section, we added the *jQuery UI* script files to the application. I did this because I want to allow the user to drag the task items around on the web page. To add the code, open the Index view of the task and add a scripts section to the code.

Listing 4-26. Scripts section in Index view

```
@section scripts {
    <script type="text/javascript">
        $(function () {
            $(".task").draggable();
        });
    </script>
}
```

Build your project and run it again. You will now be able to click the task items and drag them around on the web page.

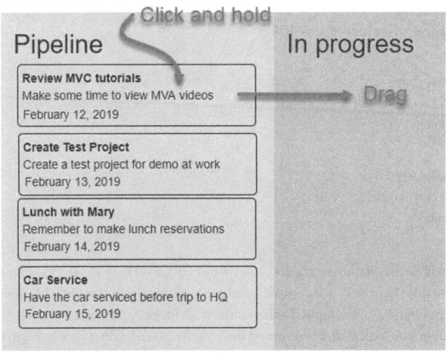

Figure 4-27. *Drag task items around*

This opens up a whole new dynamic to your web applications. Being able to add a script section to your web page gives you the ability to add additional functionality to your application that is not available out of the box.

But let's have a closer look at this @section scripts block that we added to our Index page. Swing back to the _Layout.cshtml page and scroll down to the bottom of the page. You will see the following code.

Listing 4-27. Rendering sections

```
@RenderSection("scripts", required: false)
```

The RenderSection, RenderBody, and RenderPage methods tell ASP.NET where to add specific page elements. You will see that we have set a parameter to tell ASP.NET that the scripts section is optional.

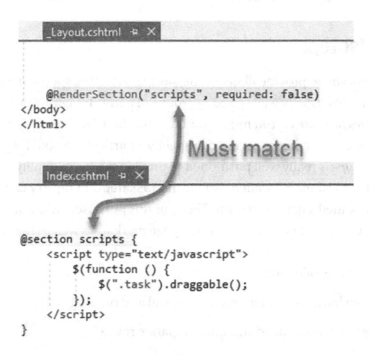

Figure 4-28. *Section names must match*

Lastly, you must remember that the section name specified in the _Layout.cshtml shared view must match the name of the section containing your script in the *Index.cshtml* view. If the names do not match, you will receive an error when running your application.

Wrapping Up

This section has taken a bit of a roundabout way to explain views, models, controllers, and Razor, but I felt that it was necessary to do this in order to give you a more whollistic view (mind the pun) of what we are discussing.

Adding a Plugin

Sometimes you might want to add additional functionality to a web application. Sure, you can definitely roll your own, but why reinvent the wheel if the functionality exists in a plugin? Let us assume that we wanted to filter our events to only display critical tasks. Critical tasks are tasks that are due within 1 day. To provide this functionality, we will look at a plugin called *Isotope* which is available from `https://isotope.metafizzy.co/`.

Installing Isotope

The plugin allows you to provide filtering and sorting as well as specify a layout mode for your items. It is especially well suited to groups of items. Imagine that you have a page that displays blog posts. You might want to filter these by date or by type (articles, podcasts, videos, etc.). Perhaps you need to specify a particular layout for your items. This is where *Isotope* is really well positioned to provide the functionality you need.

Before I can add Isotope, I want to isolate the `Task` items in my `div` column. I also need to provide something to trigger the filter. For this purpose, I will just add two buttons. This means that I need to modify my page markup as well as the *customstyles. scss* file.

We need to do the following:

- Add two buttons to filter between critical and original tasks.

- Move the column headings into a separate row.

- Specify new CSS classes for the headings.

- Modify the customstyles.scss file to style the headings.

The easiest way to illustrate these changes to the *Index* view is to summarize them in one graphic. You will see that the buttons added are standard Bootstrap buttons. Each button has been given an ID, so that we can attach a click event to these in the jQuery that will filter our tasks.

I have moved the headings into their own row, because I want the task items in a separate div. Lastly, I have added three new CSS classes to the headings. These are

- task-pipeline-heading

- task-in-progress-heading

- task-completed-heading

These allow me to target the headings specifically and apply styles to them. Modify your Index view to look the same as in Figure 4-29.

```
<button type="button" class="btn btn-primary" id="btn-order-default">Original</button>
<button type="button" class="btn btn-danger" id="btn-order-name">Critical Tasks</button>

<div class="container">            Buttons          New classes
    <div class="row">
        <div class="col-md-4 task-pipeline-heading"><h2>Pipeline</h2></div>
        <div class="col-md-4 task-in-progress-heading"><h2>In progress</h2></div>
        <div class="col-md-4 task-completed-heading"><h2>Completed</h2></div>
    </div>
    <div class="row">        New heading row
        <div class="col-md-4 task-pipeline">
            @foreach (var item in Model)
            {
                <div class="task">
                    <div class="task-id">
                        @item.TaskID
                    </div>
                    <div class="task-title">
                        @item.TaskTitle
                    </div>
                    <div class="task-body">
                        @item.TaskBody
                    </div>
                    <div class="task-date">
                        @item.DueDate.ToString("MMMM dd, yyyy")
                    </div>
                </div>
            }
        </div>
        <div class="col-md-4 task-in-progress" id="inprogress">
        </div>
        <div class="col-md-4 task-completed">
        </div>
    </div>
</div>
```

Figure 4-29. *Modified HTML*

The next thing we want to do is change the customstyles.scss file to accommodate the new classes for the headings. I will keep it really simple and just make the color the same.

We can do this by simply adding the new class names to the existing classes that implement the background color. In scss we can "chain" classes that will apply the same style to the elements on the page. You will see that the class names are separated by a comma (refer to task-pipeline and task-pipeline-heading).

Listing 4-28. Modified customstyles.scss

```scss
.task {
    border: 1px solid blue;
    border-radius: 5px;
    padding: 5px;
    margin: 5px;

    .task-id {
        display: none;
    }

    .task-title {
        font-weight: bold;
    }
}

.task-pipeline, .task-in-progress, .task-completed {
    min-height: 500px;
}

.task-pipeline, .task-pipeline-heading {
    background-color: powderblue;
}

.task-in-progress, .task-in-progress-heading {
    background-color: thistle;
    z-index: -1;
}
```

```
.task-completed, .task-completed-heading {
    background-color: plum;
    z-index: -1;
}
```

Once we have done this, we want a way to identify critical tasks. As mentioned earlier, critical tasks are due within 1 day. Here we can use Razor to perform some conditional logic to create dynamic client code. The client code we will be dynamically generating here are CSS classes.

Critical tasks will have a class of `critical` added to it. This will allow the Isotope plugin to identify the items we want to filter by.

Please note that the class you filter by can be anything you want. It can be date, name, color, type, or any other classification you need. You will be telling Isotope what the filter will be in the jQuery.

In the `foreach` loop on the *Index* page, we are going to add a condition that if the task item has a due date within a day from now, it needs to be classified as `critical`. If not, it simply does not add a class. Modify the foreach loop as follows.

Listing 4-29. Modified foreach loop

```
@foreach (var item in Model)
{
    <div class="task @(item.DueDate <= DateTime.Now.AddDays(1) ? "critical"
    : "")">
        <div class="task-id">
            @item.TaskID
        </div>
        <div class="task-title">
            @item.TaskTitle
        </div>
        <div class="task-body">
            @item.TaskBody
        </div>
```

```
    <div class="task-date">
        @item.DueDate.ToString("MMMM dd, yyyy")
    </div>
  </div>
}
```

The crux of this logic lies in the addition of the `critical` classification to certain task items. Now that we have added the code needed to correctly style and class our task items, we need to add the Isotope plugin. Swing over to the Isotope web site and download the *isotope.pkgd.min.js* file. Add this file to your *Scripts* folder.

Next, modify the `BundleConfig` class' `RegisterBundles` method, and add a `ScriptBundle` for Isotope.

Listing 4-30. Adding Isotope ScriptBundle

```
bundles.Add(new ScriptBundle("~/bundles/isotope")
    .Include("~/Scripts/isotope.pkgd.min.js"));
```

Lastly, to add this bundle to your application when it runs, you need to modify the *_Layout.cshtml* file. Just below the `@Scripts.Render` for Bootstrap, modify your code to include the Isotope bundle.

```
@Scripts.Render("~/bundles/jquery")
@Scripts.Render("~/bundles/bootstrap")
@Scripts.Render("~/bundles/isotope")          Add

@RenderSection("scripts", required: false)
</body>
</html>
```

Figure 4-30. *Add Isotope bundle*

We are now ready to add a little bit of jQuery to the Index view for tasks.

Making Isotope Work

We will be adding some jQuery to our document ready section. In jQuery we can use the shorthand code for the traditional `$(document).ready(function(){ //code });` by simply typing `$(function() { //code });` instead. Our `script` section will therefore look as follows.

Listing 4-31. Modified script section

```
<script type="text/javascript">

    var $grid;

    $(function () {
        $(".task").draggable();

        $grid = $('.task-pipeline').isotope({
            // options
            itemSelector: '.task'
        });

        $("#btn-order-default").click(function () {
            $grid = $grid.isotope({ filter: '*' });
        });

        $("#btn-order-name").click(function () {
            $grid = $grid.isotope({ filter: '.critical' });
        });
    });
</script>
```

The code might look a little confusing at first, but it is really simple to understand once we break it up into its functional parts.

```
@section scripts {
    <script type="text/javascript">

        var $grid;              Grid variable

        $(function () {
            $(".task").draggable();

Isotope container

            $grid = $('.task-pipeline').isotope({
                // options
                itemSelector: '.task'
            });
                                  Isotope items

            $("#btn-order-default").click(function () {
                $grid = $grid.isotope({ filter: '*' });
            });
            Filter by everything

            $("#btn-order-name").click(function () {
                $grid = $grid.isotope({ filter: '.critical' });
            });
        });
    </script>   Filter by critical
}
```

Figure 4-31. *Isotope logic*

We need to specify a container for the Isotope grid. This is the class of the div that contains our Task items. The containing div class for our Task items is the .task-pipeline class.

Next, we need to tell Isotope what each item class it will contain will be. In our markup, our .task-pipeline div contains multiple .task class divs. Telling Isotope what our containing class and item class are essentially instantiates the Isotope grid.

I call it a grid because, logically, that makes sense to me.

I then need to add click events for my two buttons. The first button #btn-order-default will tell the Isotope grid to filter by all the items it contains.

You will notice that some elements are referred to by class names (e.g., .task and .task-pipeline), while other elements are referred to by their IDs (e.g., #btn-order-default). In jQuery, if you reference the ID of an element, you use a #[ID] sign. If you refer to the class, you use the period[classname].

The second button #btn-order-name will only display .task items that also have a class of critical. Having a look at the generated HTML, we can see that there are only two tasks marked as critical.

```
▼<div class="row"> == $0
    ::before
  ▼<div class="col-md-4 task-pipeline" style="position:
  relative; height: 328px;">
    ▶<div class="task critical ui-draggable ui-draggable-
    handle" style="position: absolute; left: 15px; top: 0px;">
    …</div>
    ▶<div class="task critical ui-draggable ui-draggable-
    handle" style="position: absolute; left: 15px; top: 82px;
    ">…</div>
    ▶<div class="task ui-draggable ui-draggable-handle"
    style="position: absolute; left: 15px; top: 164px;">…
    </div>
    ▶<div class="task ui-draggable ui-draggable-handle"
    style="position: absolute; left: 15px; top: 246px;">…
    </div>
  </div>
  <div class="col-md-4 task-in-progress" id="inprogress">
          </div>
  <div class="col-md-4 task-completed">
          </div>
    ::after
</div>
```

Figure 4-32. *Generated HTML*

Run your application and you will see that the four task items are displayed. If you click the *Critical Tasks* button, you will see the items filter to show only the critical tasks.

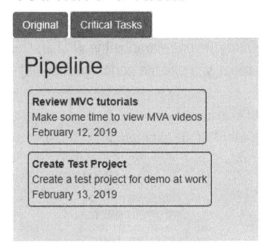

Figure 4-33. *Filtered by critical tasks*

When you click the *Original* button, the task list is reset and shows all the tasks.

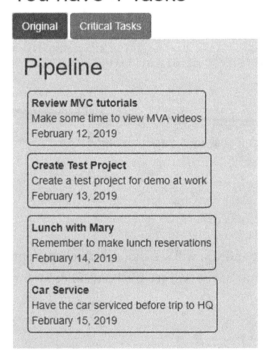

Figure 4-34. *Original tasks displayed*

The Isotope plugin provides a rich set of additional functionalities to your web applications. Here we only looked at filtering, but it is equally good at sorting items and even has specific ways to provide a fluid layout for your items.

This is the power of plugins in general. You can add functionality to your web application by using well-supported, well-designed plugins that save you the trouble of having to code that functionality yourself.

Testing Your Responsive Layout Using Chrome

The Google Chrome browser has definitely become one of the most popular browsers in the world today. The power of being able to add functionality to the browser with extensions allows users to make it their own. For developers, it also provides a host of features in the form of Chrome's Developer Tools. We will be looking at one portion of it in this section called the device toolbar. This helps developers test the responsiveness of your web application layout across multiple devices.

Starting with the Developer Tools

To start using the developer tools, hold down *Ctrl+Shift+I* or right-click your web page and select *Inspect* from the context menu.

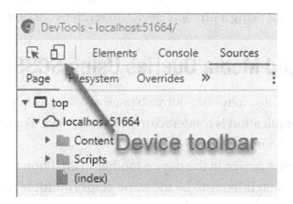

Figure 4-35. *Chrome DevTools*

At the top-left corner, you will see the icon for the device toolbar toggle. Clicking this will display your web page as if it was being viewed on a mobile device.

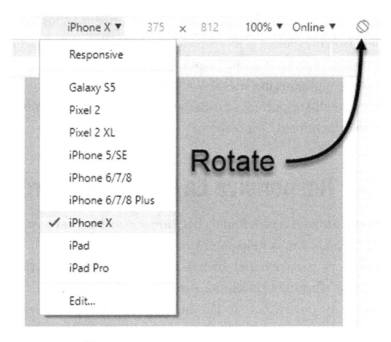

Figure 4-36. *Device toolbar*

The device toolbar allows us to select a specific mobile device to view the page as. Another great feature of it is the ability to rotate your web page, as if it is being viewed on a mobile device in a rotated manner.

This is probably the closest you will come to being able to render your web page on multiple devices without using a physical device to render your page on.

Breakpoints and Media Queries Using SCSS

Now that we have seen how to render our web page across multiple devices, it's time to see how our web application is rendered on mobile devices. For this example, I have simply chosen to use the iPhone X.

When we change the device in the device toolbar to an iPhone X, we see that there is a problem. The problem is likely to be the same across multiple mobile devices (excluding tablets).

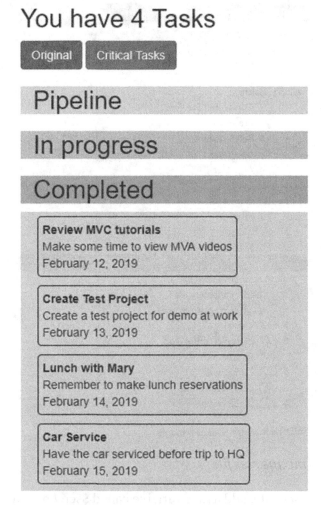

Figure 4-37. *Incorrect mobile layout*

The heading divs I created earlier are stacking incorrectly. In truth, the stacking is 100% correct, because this is how the Bootstrap system works. It is however not what we want for our web application.

The way we can fix this is to use breakpoints and media queries. What these allow us to do is specify certain styles in our generated CSS for specific mobile devices.

I'm not going to fix this issue, I'm merely going to hide the headings when viewed on a mobile device. This will illustrate the use of breakpoints and media queries and how they work. Start off by creating a new file called *_mixins.scss* in your *scss* folder.

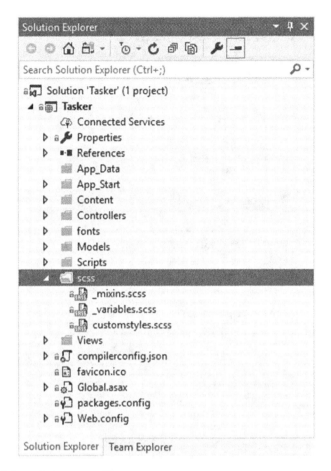

Figure 4-38. *Add _mixins.scss file*

In your _variables.scss file, add a new variable called $screen-mobile-max and set it as follows.

Listing 4-32. New variable

```
$screen-mobile-max: 414px;
```

Now edit the new *_mixins.scss* file and add the following code to it.

Listing 4-33. Add mixin

```
@import "_variables.scss";

@mixin mobile {
    @media (max-width: #{$screen-mobile-max}) {
```

```
    @content;
  }
}
```

Because we are using our new variable in the mixin, we need to import the *_variables.scss* file. Now save your project to compile your code. Then edit the customstyles.scss file and add the following media query to it to target mobile devices.

Listing 4-34. Target mobile devices

```
@include mobile {
    .task-pipeline-heading, .task-in-progress-heading, .task-completed-
    heading {
        display: none;
    }
}
```

What this does is target mobile devices up until a max width of 414px and then applies the display: none style to the column headings. This will then hide the column headings on mobile devices. If the screen width exceeds 414px, then the column headers will be displayed again.

This allows you to play around with your media queries and apply specific styles targeting specific mobile devices.

Debugging Your jQuery Using Chrome Developer Tools

Being able to debug your jQuery and JavaScript gives you complete control over the code you write. No more guessing and hit and miss attempts at debugging errors (here's looking at you SYSPRO VbScript devs). You can write your jQuery and use Chrome Developer Tools with complete confidence to debug your code.

What I would like to do is allow the user to check off certain tasks and mark them as completed. For this I will need a checkbox on my task that has the text *Mark completed*. When the user checks this checkbox, the text must change to *Completed* and the task element on the page should change to green. This is all possible with jQuery. The first thing I want to do is set all the .task elements to a transparent background color. I want to be able to just uncheck the task and, on the uncheck, set the color to transparent. Modify the *customstyles.scss* file and add a background-color: transparent property to the .task class.

Listing 4-35. Customstyles for Task element

```
.task {
    border: 1px solid blue;
    border-radius: 5px;
    padding: 5px;
    margin: 5px;
    background-color: transparent;

    .task-id {
        display: none;
    }

    .task-title {
        font-weight: bold;
    }
}
```

The next thing I want to do is add a checkbox to my tasks and give it a unique ID.

Listing 4-36. Modified task item

```
@{ var iCount = 0; }
@foreach (var item in Model)
{
    iCount += 1;
    <div class="task @(item.DueDate <= DateTime.Now.AddDays(1) ? "critical"
    : "")">
        <div class="task-id">
            @item.TaskID
        </div>
        <div class="task-title">
            @item.TaskTitle
        </div>
```

```
    <div class="task-body">
        @item.TaskBody
    </div>
    <div class="task-date">
        @item.DueDate.ToString("MMMM dd, yyyy")
    </div>
    <div class="form-check">
        <input type="checkbox" class="form-check-input"
        id="chkCompleted@(iCount)">
        <label class="form-check-label" for="chkCompleted@(iCount)"
        id="chkLabel@(iCount)">Mark completed</label>
    </div>
    </div>
}
```

What I have done is declared a counter called iCount that I increment on each iteration. I then concatenate this value to the checkbox ID to ensure that the checkbox element's ID is unique. I do the same for the label element.

Figure 4-39. *Set unique IDs*

Save your changes and run your application and look at the task items. They will all have checkboxes added to them with the text Mark completed.

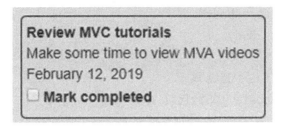

Figure 4-40. *Task item with checkbox*

If we look at the generated code for our task item, we will see that the IDs are indeed unique.

```
<div class="task critical">
    <div class="task-id">
        1
    </div>
    <div class="task-title">
        Review MVC tutorials
    </div>
    <div class="task-body">
        Make some time to view MVA videos
    </div>
    <div class="task-date">
        February 12, 2019
    </div>
    <div class="form-check">
        <input type="checkbox"
                class="form-check-input"
                id="chkCompleted1">
        <label class="form-check-label"
                for="chkCompleted1"
                id="chkLabel1">
        Mark completed
        </label>
    </div>
</div>
```

Figure 4-41. *Generated client code for a task*

We are now ready to write some jQuery. It is here that we are faced with our first challenge. We do not know how many tasks we are going to have. Therefore, we do not know what the IDs will be for the checkboxes. We need to add an event when the user checks a checkbox, but in order to do this, we need to know the ID of that checkbox. Those IDs we add dynamically using the iCount variable.

This is where we will be using some jQuery selectors and fancy tricks to get to the elements we want.

Please note that the code I am about to add contains a bug. The purpose of this section is to illustrate debugging using DevTools.

Go ahead and add the following jQuery to the script section of your Index view.

Listing 4-37. jQuery code to mark completed items

```
$('[id^="chkCompleted"]').click(function () {
    var $div = $(this).closest('div');

    if (this.checked) {
        $("label[for='" + this.id + "']")["0"].innerText = "Completed";
        $div.css("background-color","#89ea31");
    }
    else {
        $("label[for='" + this.id + "']")["0"].innerText = "Mark completed";
        $div.css("background-color","transparent");
    }
});
```

Let's break this up and explain them a bit. The code in the image in Figure 4-42 is exactly the same as in Listing 4-37.

```
$('[id^="chkCompleted"]').click(function () {        1
    var $div = $(this).closest('div');              2

    if (this.checked) {        3

        $("label[for='" + this.id + "']")["0"]        4
            .innerText = "Completed";
    5   $div.css("background-color","#89ea31");
    }
    else {
    6   $("label[for='" + this.id + "']")["0"]
            .innerText = "Mark completed";
        $div.css("background-color","transparent");        7
    }
});
```

Figure 4-42. *jQuery logic*

The logic corresponds to the steps in the preceding image and is as follows:

1. For all elements with an ID starting with the text *chkCompleted*, add a click event.

2. Find a reference to the closest div element.

3. If the checkbox has been checked...

4. Get the label element with the for attribute equal to the ID of the checkbox, and set its text to *Completed*.

5. Use the div reference we found earlier, and set the background color to green.

6. If the checkbox is unchecked, reset the label element with the for attribute equal to the ID of the checkbox back to the original text.

7. Use the div reference we found earlier, and set the background color to transparent.

We seem to be in business, so let's run our application and test our jQuery.

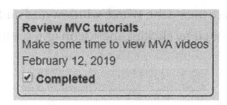

Figure 4-43. *Checking the task item checkbox*

Unfortunately, we have hit a snag. While the check event works and the checkbox label's text is correctly changed, the entire task item's background color isn't being set to green. To see what is going on, hold down *Ctrl+Shift+I* or right-click your web page and select *Inspect* from the context menu. Select the *Sources* tab and scroll to the jQuery code on your *Index* page.

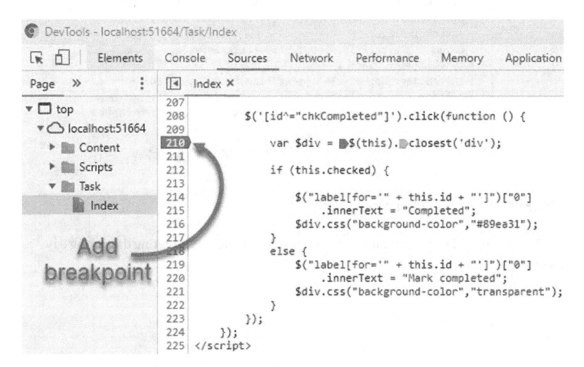

Figure 4-44. *Add breakpoint on jQuery code*

With the breakpoint added, check and uncheck your task item checkbox. You will see that the breakpoint is hit and your web page enters a paused state on each check and uncheck action.

While the code is paused, locate the *Watch* window and add the expression $(this).closest('div') to a new watch by clicking the + icon and pasting the expression into the textbox provided.

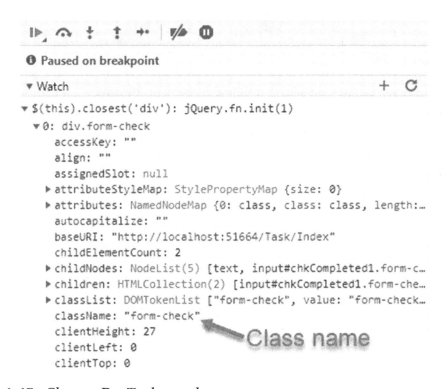

Figure 4-45. *Chrome DevTools watch*

Immediately, I can see what the problem is. Our jQuery is targeting the wrong div element.

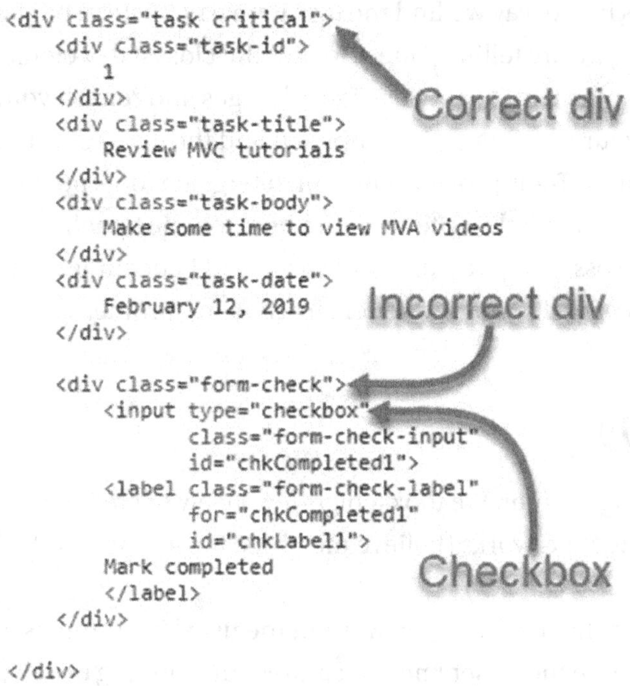

```
<div class="task critical">
    <div class="task-id">
        1
    </div>
    <div class="task-title">
        Review MVC tutorials
    </div>
    <div class="task-body">
        Make some time to view MVA videos
    </div>
    <div class="task-date">
        February 12, 2019
    </div>

    <div class="form-check">
        <input type="checkbox"
            class="form-check-input"
            id="chkCompleted1">
        <label class="form-check-label"
            for="chkCompleted1"
            id="chkLabel1">
        Mark completed
        </label>
    </div>

</div>
```

Correct div

Incorrect div

Checkbox

Figure 4-46. *Location of correct and incorrect divs*

We are targeting the closest div element instead of the div that holds our task item. Modify your jQuery as follows.

Listing 4-38. Correct jQuery code

```
$('[id^="chkCompleted"]').click(function () {
    var $div = $(this).closest('div[class^="task"]');

    if (this.checked) {
        $("label[for='" + this.id + "']")["0"]
            .innerText = "Completed";
        $div.css("background-color","#89ea31");
    }
    else {
        $("label[for='" + this.id + "']")["0"]
            .innerText = "Mark completed";
        $div.css("background-color","transparent");
    }
});
```

The change lies in the way we find the task item `div`. Instead of just finding the closest `div` element, we are telling jQuery to find the closest `div` element that also has a class that starts with the text "`task`". Save four changes and refresh your web page. This time, if you check your task item, it is completed and the task item changes to green.

Chrome Developer Tools provide a host of debugging tools not even mentioned in this chapter. You can definitely write an entire book on the benefits of using Chrome DevTools. Nevertheless, we have run out of space and I encourage you to have a closer look at the features provided for developers by Google Chrome.

Wrapping Up

Phew, this was a long chapter. We took a high-level view of creating an ASP.NET MVC application and how MVC works (believe me, there is a lot more to MVC than discussed in this chapter).

The focus of this chapter, however, was not the usual MVC topics. I wanted to take you further and explore the lesser known features surrounding developing responsive web applications and styling those applications easily.

We had a look at how we reference jQuery and Bootstrap, before we looked at how to set up and use scss to style our web pages. We saw that scss compiles down to CSS and that scss is syntactically similar to C#.

Then we had a brief look at what models, controllers, and views are and how to use Razor inside your view. The power of Razor is evident in the fact that we can dynamically create client code based on logic coming from a database, for example.

We had a look at how we can extend the functionality of our web application by adding a plugin called Isotope. It provided filtering for us out of the box, freeing us from having to roll our own.

Lastly, we had a look at testing the responsive layout of our web application across various mobile devices. What's more, we did so right from within Google Chrome Developer Tools. We also saw how we can debug our jQuery code using the Watch window in the DevTools console.

In the next chapter, we will be looking at .NET Core and figure out exactly what all the fuss is about, so stay tuned.

CHAPTER 5

Getting Started with .NET Core 3.0

These days it's hard to code using the Microsoft technology stack without hearing the word .NET Core. It might leave some wondering exactly what it is. Well, .NET Core is an open source development platform that is maintained on GitHub by Microsoft and the .NET Community. It allows developers to write applications that support Windows, Linux, and macOS. In fact, .NET Core can be summarized by the following characteristics:

- It is cross-platform, running on macOS, Windows, and Linux.

- It is open source, using MIT and Apache 2 licenses, and is also a .NET Foundation project (`https://dotnetfoundation.org/About`).

- It executes code exactly the same across multiple architectures that include x86, x64, and ARM.

- It allows the use of command-line tools for local development.

- It can be used with Docker containers, installed side-by-side or included in your app, making .NET Core deployment very flexible.

- .NET Core compatibility extends to Mono, Xamarin, and the .NET Framework via the .NET Standard.

- It is supported by Microsoft per .NET Core Support (`https://dotnet.microsoft.com/platform/support/policy/dotnet-core`).

© Dirk Strauss 2019
D. Strauss, *Exploring Advanced Features in C#*, https://doi.org/10.1007/978-1-4842-4856-0_5

We also need to have a look at the composition of .NET Core. It is composed of the following:

- The .NET Core runtime (available on GitHub at `https://github.com/dotnet/coreclr`). It includes garbage collection, JIT compiler, primitive classes, and low-level classes.

- The ASP.NET runtime (available on GitHub at `https://github.com/aspnet/AspNetCore`). This allows you to build cloud-based web applications on Windows, Mac, or Linux.

- The .NET Core CLI tools (available on GitHub at `https://github.com/dotnet/cli`).

- The dotnet tool that launches .NET Core apps and CLI tools.

In this chapter, we are going to take a look at creating and running .NET Core applications using .NET Core 3.0 Preview 2 and Visual Studio 2019 Preview. We will be talking about

- Creating .NET Core apps in Visual Studio 2019

- What is new in .NET Core 3.0

- Installing .NET Core 3.0 Preview on Linux with Snap

- Creating and running an ASP.NET MVC app on Linux

- Editing your ASP.NET Core MVC app on Linux with Visual Studio Code

- Debugging your ASP.NET Core MVC project with Visual Studio Code

Before we can jump in, you need to ensure that you have downloaded and installed .NET Core 3.0 on your system. Head on over to this URL and download the installer for your platform: `https://dotnet.microsoft.com/download/dotnet-core/3.0`

Creating .NET Core Apps in Visual Studio 2019

Once you have installed .NET Core 3.0, we can start creating applications. I have just created a simple .NET Core Console application. When the project is created, ensure that you are targeting the .NET Core 3.0 framework from the project properties page (Figure 5-1).

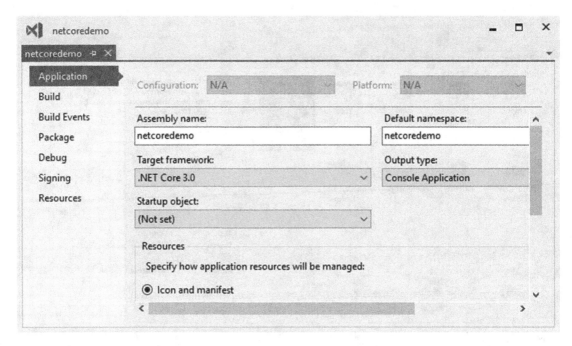

Figure 5-1. *Target .NET Core 3.0*

I am not going to go into any detail on how to create a .NET Core Console application. The point here is to show you how to target .NET Core 3.0.

When creating ASP.NET Core applications, ensure that you select ASP.NET Core 3.0 from the dropdown (Figure 5-2).

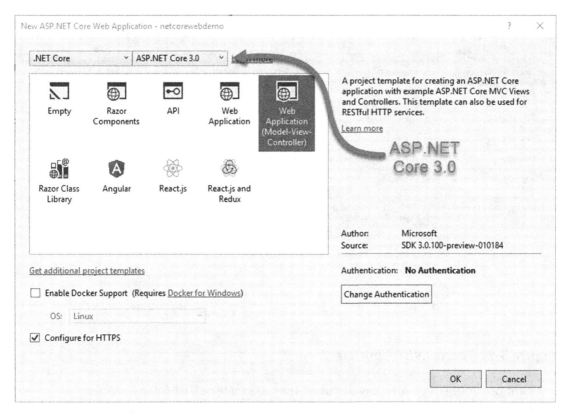

Figure 5-2. *Create ASP.NET Core 3.0 app*

My solution in Visual Studio now contains two projects as seen in Figure 5-3. These are a .NET Core Console application and an ASP.NET Core MVC application.

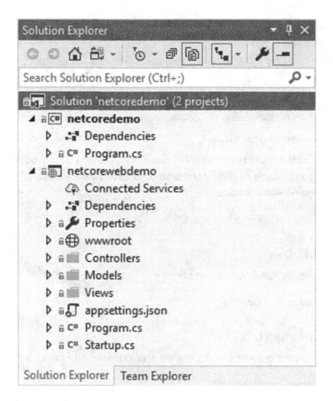

Figure 5-3. *Solution Explorer*

With the two application templates created, let's have a look at what .NET Core 3.0 can offer developers.

What Is New in .NET Core 3.0

There are a host of new features in .NET Core 3.0, some of which I will not discuss. I will, however, highlight some of the more interesting features.

Windows Desktop

With the release of .NET Core 3.0, you can now create Windows desktop applications using Windows Forms and WPF as can be seen in Figure 5-4. If you add a new project to your solution, and filter by .NET Core, you will notice that you have two new templates you can choose from.

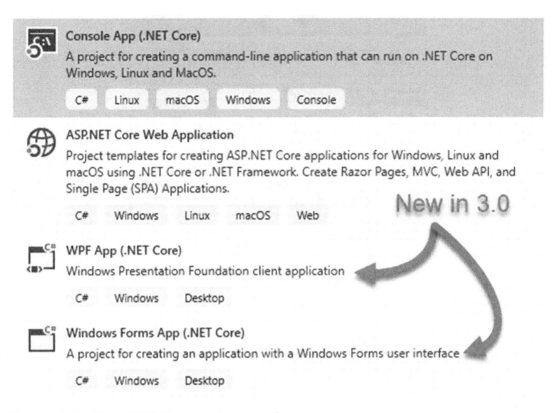

Figure 5-4. *New .NET Core project templates*

The first two version iterations of .NET Core supported web applications and APIs, IoT, and Console applications.

Please note that even though .NET Core 3.0 adds support for building Windows desktop apps using WinForms and WPF, you will still only be able to run these apps on Windows.

Because Entity Framework is used by many desktop apps, .NET Core 3.0 also supports Entity Framework 6. Visual Studio 2019 gives you the ability to create WinForm and WPF apps, but you can do the same thing with dotnet new in the command line. To create a new .NET Core app for WPF and WinForms, you can run the following commands from the command line.

Listing 5-1. Using dotnet new in the command line

```
dotnet new wpf
dotnet new winforms
```

See how easy that is? In fact, a look at the command line shows the screenshot in Figure 5-5.

Figure 5-5. *New WinForms app with dotnet new*

If we now swing over the folder that we created, we can see the solution files created by dotnet new (Figure 5-6).

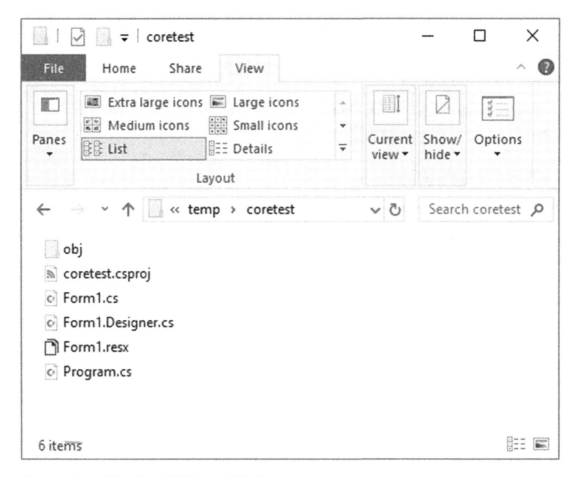

Figure 5-6. *Files for .NET Core WinForm app*

You can now run your new WinForms application by typing `dotnet run` in the command line. It might take a few seconds to compile and display your application, but soon you will see the .NET Core WinForm app as displayed in Figure 5-7.

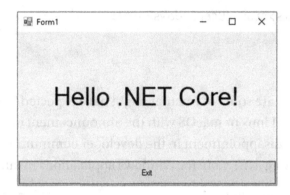

Figure 5-7. *Running the .NET Core WinForms app*

If you look at the folder that you used to create the application in, you will notice that there is now a bin folder added. When creating .NET Core Console applications, the project targets the `Microsoft.NET.Sdk` SDK. You will see this if you view the *netcoredemo. csproj* file of the .NET Core Console application we created at the beginning of this chapter.

Listing 5-2. .NET Core Console csproj file

```
<Project Sdk="Microsoft.NET.Sdk">

  <PropertyGroup>
    <OutputType>Exe</OutputType>
    <TargetFramework>netcoreapp3.0</TargetFramework>
  </PropertyGroup>

</Project>
```

The .NET Core WinForms app uses a different SDK (which the WPF app incidentally also uses), but also declares which UI framework it uses.

The .NET Core WPF application will declare a `<UseWPF>true</UseWPF>` property in the csproj file, while the .NET Core WinForms app will declare a `<UseWindowsForms>true</UseWindowsForms>` property in the csproj file.

Listing 5-3. .NET Core WinForms csproj file

```
<Project Sdk="Microsoft.NET.Sdk.WindowsDesktop">

  <PropertyGroup>
    <OutputType>WinExe</OutputType>
    <TargetFramework>netcoreapp3.0</TargetFramework>
```

```
  <UseWindowsForms>true</UseWindowsForms>
 </PropertyGroup>
```

```
</Project>
```

I am sure that there are some of you that might have expected WinForms and WPF desktop apps to run on Linux or macOS with the announcement of .NET Core 3.0. There does seem to be some disappointment in the developer community regarding this. The benefits, though, of using .NET Core for Windows applications mean that we have

- Improved performance

- Benefits provided by being open source

- Ability to install multiple .NET Core versions side-by-side

- Ability to publish self-contained apps

- Access to .NET Core only features (e.g., Span<T>)

Yeah, they had me at *Improved Performance*. As you know .NET Core is open source, but *WPF*, *Windows Forms*, and *WinUI* have also been open-sourced. Find them here on GitHub:

- WPF: https://github.com/dotnet/wpf

- Windows Forms: https://github.com/dotnet/winforms

- Windows UI: https://github.com/Microsoft/microsoft-ui-xaml

As .NET Core evolves, we are sure to see more support for APIs typically used in Windows desktop apps.

Support for C# 8.0

Think back to Chapter 3 where we discussed C# 8.0. The features available to developers are now available in .NET Core 3.0. With each new preview that is released, more C# 8.0 features are being introduced.

It would only make sense to do this, because having C# 8.0 available elsewhere and not in .NET Core would be somewhat frustrating. Have a read through Chapter 3 (if not done so already) and see what C# 8.0 offers you in the line of improvements to the language.

Default Executables

For applications that use a globally installed version of .NET Core, they are built with a default exe. Before this, you only had an exe with self-contained applications. This means that you can double-click the exe or start it from the command line without using the dotnet tool.

On Windows

On Windows you would do the following to create a new directory in the *c:\temp* folder, create a new .NET Core Console application and run it.

Listing 5-4.   Creating a .NET Core Console app on Windows

```
cd c:\temp
md coreconsoletest
cd c:\temp\coreconsoletest
c:\temp\coreconsoletest>dotnet new console
dotnet build
cd c:\temp\coreconsoletest\bin\debug\netcoreapp3.0
coreconsoletest.exe
```

If you run your exe, you will see that the text *Hello World!* is output in the console window as seen in Figure 5-8. Running the dll via *dotnet* produces the same result.

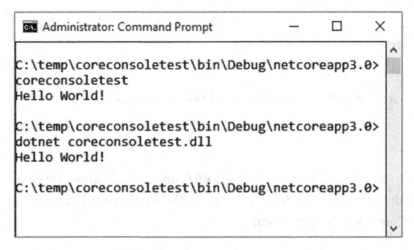

Figure 5-8.   *Running the default exe and dll*

On macOS

We can do the same thing on macOS. Be sure to download .NET Core 3.0 Preview and install it on macOS. Next, open Terminal.

In Terminal, I create a folder on my Desktop called *netcoremac* and then change to that directory. I then create a new .NET Core Console application in the directory and build it. Then I change directory to where the executable is located, which is the *netcoreapp3.0* directory.

Listing 5-5. Creating a .NET Core Console app on macOS

```
mkdir ~/Desktop/netcoremac
cd ~/Desktop/netcoremac
dotnet new console
dotnet build
cd ~/Desktop/netcoremac/bin/Debug/netcoreapp3.0
```

I am then able to run the *netcoremac* executable with ./netcoremac as well as the netcoremac.dll with the dotnet command as seen in Figure 5-9.

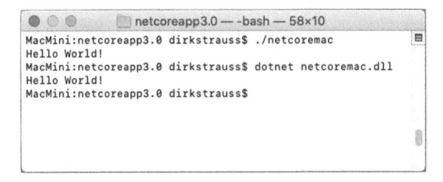

Figure 5-9. *Running the default executable and dll on macOS*

On Linux

On Linux, the same is true for a new .NET Core Console application. Open up Terminal and create a directory called *netcorelinux* on the Desktop. Inside that directory, I created a new .NET Core Console application.

Listing 5-6. Creating a .NET Core Console app on Linux

```
cd ~/Desktop
mkdir netcorelinux
cd netcorelinux
dotnet new console
dotnet build
cd ~/Desktop/netcorelinux/bin/Debug/netcoreapp3.0
```

I can use the same commands that I used on macOS to run the default executable. Run the command `./netcorelinux` to run the default executable and then run the command `dotnet netcorelinux.dll` to run the dll. The output is seen in Figure 5-10.

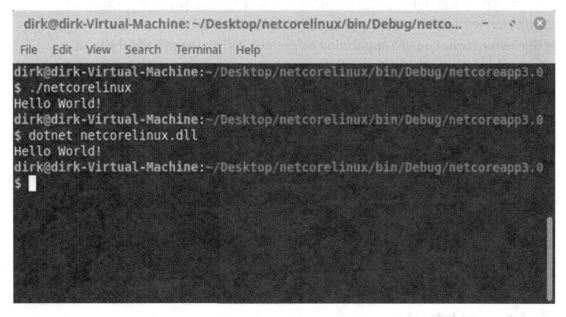

Figure 5-10. *Running the default executable and dll on Linux*

Fast Built-In JSON Support

JSON has become almost essential as part of modern .NET development. The go-to library is Json.Net. Starting with .NET Core 3.0, three main JSON-related types have been added to the `System.Text.Json` namespace to provide built-in JSON support. These are

- System.Text.Json.Utf8JsonReader

- System.Text.Json.Utf8JsonWriter

- System.Text.Json.JsonDocument

This means that the new built-in JSON support provides high performance and low allocation and is based on Span<byte>. You can read more about Span<T> here: https://docs.microsoft.com/en-us/dotnet/api/system.span-1

Cryptography

The System.Security.Cryptography.AesGcm and System.Security.Cryptography. AesCcm namespaces add support for AES-GCM and AES-CCM ciphers. These are the first authenticated encryption algorithms added to .NET Core. Let's have a look at the *netcoredemo* console application we created earlier. We will add the basic encryption and decryption methods. Ensure that you have added the System.Security. Cryptography namespace.

Listing 5-7. AES-GCM encryption method

```
public static byte[] Encrypt(out byte[] key, out byte[] nonce, out byte[]
tag, byte[] dataToEncrypt)
{
    key = new byte[16];
    nonce = new byte[12];
    RandomNumberGenerator.Fill(key);
    RandomNumberGenerator.Fill(nonce);

    tag = new byte[16];
    byte[] ciphertext = new byte[dataToEncrypt.Length];

    using (AesGcm aes = new AesGcm(key))
        aes.Encrypt(nonce, dataToEncrypt, ciphertext, tag);

    return ciphertext;
}
```

We are using out parameters to pass the key, nonce, and tag values back to the calling code.

When working with cryptography, we create a nonce which is a random value that is used to prevent replay attacks. This is if someone intercepts the first message and tries to send the message a second time. The nonce for each message must be unique. If the receiving application receives a duplicate nonce, it knows that it needs to discard the message.

The encrypted data is returned to the calling code and passed to the Decrypt method.

Listing 5-8. AES-GCM decryption method

```
public static void Decrypt(byte[] key, byte[] nonce, byte[] tag, byte[]
ciphertext)
{
    byte[] decryptedData = new byte[ciphertext.Length];
    using (AesGcm aes = new AesGcm(key))
        aes.Decrypt(nonce, ciphertext, tag, decryptedData);

    string decryptedText = Encoding.UTF8.GetString(decryptedData);
    Console.WriteLine(decryptedText);
}
```

The calling code will then call the Encrypt and Decrypt methods as follows.

Listing 5-9. Calling Encrypt and Decrypt

```
byte[] dataToEncrypt = Encoding.UTF8.GetBytes("String to encrypt");

var encrData = Encrypt(out byte[] key, out byte[] nonce, out byte[] tag,
dataToEncrypt);
Decrypt(key, nonce, tag, encrData);
Console.ReadLine();
```

Running the application, you will see the decrypted text displayed in the decryptedText variable. See Figure 5-11 where I have inspected the variable.

```
1 reference | 0 changes | 0 authors, 0 changes
public static void Decrypt(byte[] key
    , byte[] nonce, byte[] tag
    , byte[] ciphertext)
{
    byte[] decryptedData = new byte[ciphertext.Length];
    using (AesGcm aes = new AesGcm(key))
        aes.Decrypt(nonce, ciphertext, tag, decryptedData);

    string decryptedText = Encoding.UTF8.GetString(decryptedData);
    Console.WriteLine(decryptedText);
}               decryptedText   ♪ ▾ "String to encrypt"
```

Figure 5-11. *Decrypted text*

If you wanted to implement the AES-CCM cipher, you would essentially do the same thing, just with a different class name (AesCcm).

Installing .NET Core 3.0 Preview on Linux with Snap

The recommended way to install .NET Core 3.0 Preview on Linux is via Snap. At the time this chapter was written, the following Linux distros support Snap:

- Arch Linux
- Debian
- Deepin
- Elementary OS
- Fedora
- GalliumOS
- KDE Neon
- Kubuntu
- Linux Mint
- Lubuntu
- Manjaro Linux
- openSUSE
- Parrot Security OS

- Raspbian

- Solus

- Ubuntu

- Xubuntu

- Zorin OS

For my purposes, I used Linux Mint. After configuring Snap on your Linux system, run the following command to install the .NET Core 3.0 Preview.

Listing 5-10. Install .NET Core 3.0 Preview with Snap

```
sudo snap install dotnet-sdk --beta --classic
```

This now makes the default .NET Core command `dotnet-sdk.dotnet` when installed via Snap. This is a namespace command and will not conflict with a globally installed .NET Core version you might have on your Linux system. I preferred to use the default `dotnet` command, seeing as this was only a test installation of Linux that I used.

To do this, you can create an alias for your `dotnet-sdk.dotnet` command by running the following in Terminal.

Listing 5-11. Creating the dotnet alias

```
sudo snap alias dotnet-sdk.dotnet dotnet
```

For more information on setting up .NET Core on Linux, refer to the following link: `https://github.com/dotnet/core/blob/master/Documentation/linux-setup.md`.

Create and Run an ASP.NET MVC App on Linux

Create a new folder on your Linux desktop. For my purposes, I am using Linux Mint. Open Terminal and navigate to the new folder you created. To see which templates are available to you, type the following command in Terminal.

Listing 5-12. Listing the dotnet new templates

```
dotnet new -l
```

This now lists all the available project templates that you can create using the `dotnet new` command.

Please note that I aliased my `dotnet-sdk.dotnet` command with `dotnet` by typing `sudo snap alias dotnet-sdk.dotnet dotnet` earlier on after installing the .NET Core 3.0 Preview on my copy of Linux Mint.

One of the templates listed is an ASP.NET Core MVC app. To create this project type, run the following command in Terminal while inside the directory you created on the Desktop earlier.

Listing 5-13. Create a .NET Core MVC app on Linux

```
dotnet new mvc
```

This will go ahead and create your ASP.NET Core MVC application in the folder we created earlier.

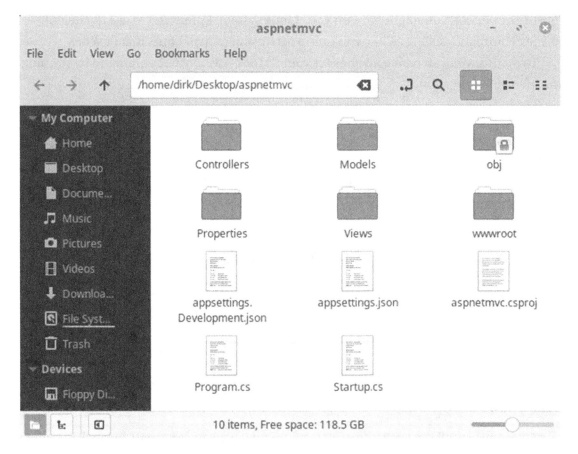

Figure 5-12. *ASP.NET Core MVC project*

Opening up the folder, you will notice that we have all the familiar files (Figure 5-12) we usually see in Visual Studio.

If you encounter an *Access to path* error on a *.nuget/packages* folder or a *Permission denied* error on the *csproj* file when creating the MVC app, run `sudo dotnet restore` and type in your password when prompted.

To run your new ASP.NET Core MVC application, type the following command in Terminal.

Listing 5-14. Running your ASP.NET Core MVC app

```
dotnet run
```

You will see that the Terminal displays some info messages. One of those messages should say *Now listening on: https://localhost:[port]* where the [port] is a valid port number. Type that URL into your browser (I used Firefox), and you will see your ASP.NET Core MVC application running on Linux as seen in Figure 5-13.

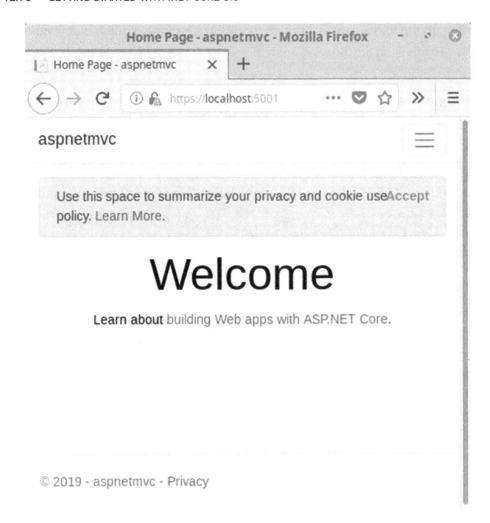

Figure 5-13. *ASP.NET Core MVC app in Firefox on Linux*

This whole process didn't even take us 2 minutes to create a project and run it on Linux.

Edit Your ASP.NET Core MVC App on Linux with Visual Studio Code

Microsoft has done a huge amount of work to bring Visual Studio to all platforms. Visual Studio Code gives developers a fantastic IDE for creating applications on Linux and macOS. I even use it daily on my Windows machine if I need to quickly work on a file.

Visual Studio Code can be downloaded from the following URL: `https://code.visualstudio.com/`. The benefits of using Visual Studio Code are

- It is a free IDE, which makes it perfect for developers wanting to try out something new.

- It is also open source. You can view the repository here on GitHub: `https://github.com/Microsoft/vscode`.

- It runs on Windows, macOS, and Linux.

This now means that I can edit my ASP.NET Core MVC project inside Visual Studio Code on Linux.

Editing Your Project

I have downloaded and installed Visual Studio Code on my installation of Linux Mint. Let's use it to open our ASP.NET Core MVC application and modify the *Index.cshtml* file for the *HomeController*. Start by opening Visual Studio Code and clicking Explorer or by pressing *Ctrl+Shift+E*. Figure 5-14 shows where you can find Explorer in Visual Studio Code.

Figure 5-14. *Open Visual Studio Code Explorer*

Click Open Folder and then open the top-level folder of your project. You will see the project files as displayed in Figure 5-15.

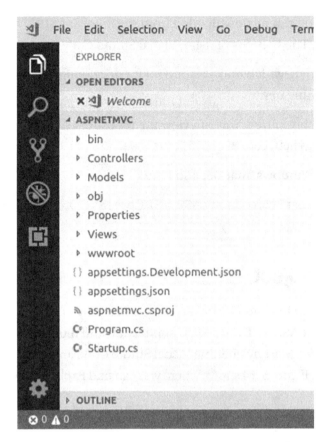

Figure 5-15. *Open project in Visual Studio Code*

In the *Views* folder, select the *Home* folder and click *Index.cshtml*. This will open the file in the code editor. Modify your code as follows.

Listing 5-15. The Index.cshtml view

```
@{
    ViewData["Title"] = "Home Page";
    var longAgoDate = DateTime.Today.AddYears(-100);
    var longDayOfWeek = longAgoDate.DayOfWeek;
}

<div class="text-center">
    <h1 class="display-4">Welcome</h1>
```

```
<h2 class="display-4">100 Years ago was @longDayOfWeek, @longAgoDate.
ToString("MMMM dd, yyyy")</h2>
</div>
```

Save the changes to your file, and then in Terminal, type in the dotnet build command and then dotnet run. Run your app in Firefox (Figure 5-16).

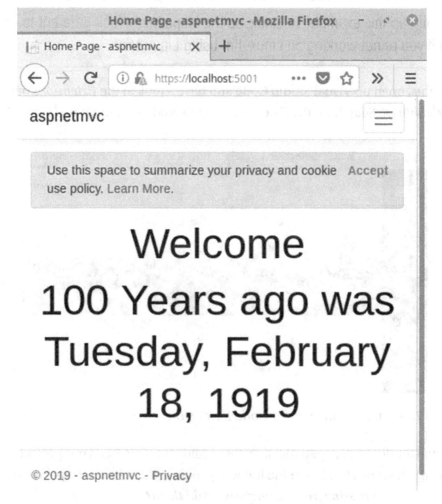

Figure 5-16. Modified ASP.NET Core MVC project

Debug Your ASP.NET Core MVC Project with Visual Studio Code

Visual Studio Code allows you to debug your code. You need to do a little heavy lifting to get this all set up, but once you have done this, you're all sorted.

I am setting up this example on Linux, so the steps might look different to your system if you're not working on Linux. I'm using Linux Mint.

To do this, open up Visual Studio Code and have a look at the *Extensions* pane or hold down *Ctrl+Shift+X*. Search for the C# extension powered by OmniSharp (Figure 5-17).

Figure 5-17. *C# for Visual Studio Code Extension*

In Visual Studio Code, open the *aspnetmvc* folder you created your project in earlier. When you do this, you should see the following message displayed: *Required assets to build and debug are missing from 'aspnetmvc'. Add them?*

When you click Yes, Visual Studio Code will add a *.vscode* (Figure 5-18) folder to your project.

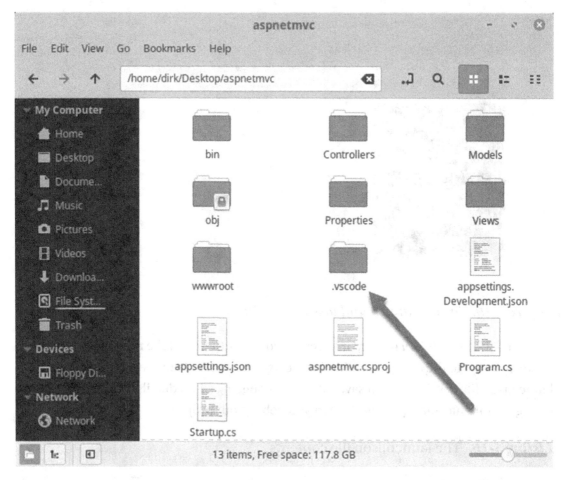

Figure 5-18. *Ensure a .vscode folder exists*

Inside this *.vscode* folder, you will see that there should be two files created by Visual Studio Code. These files are

- launch.json

- tasks.json

You will need these files (Figure 5-19) in order to debug your ASP.NET Core MVC application. If these files do not exist, delete the *.vscode* folder and restart Visual Studio Code and open the *aspnetmvc* project folder again.

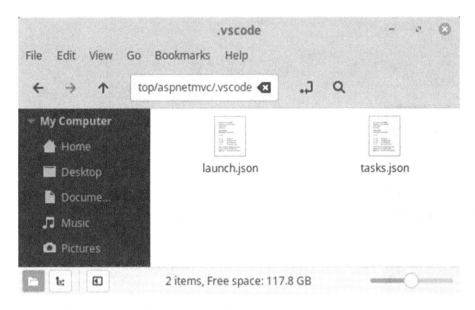

Figure 5-19. *Ensure launch and tasks files exist*

Open the *launch.json* file and inspect the contents thereof. Take note that the path needs to be set to the correct location for the *aspnetcore.dll* file in the bin folder. The launch.json file configures and saves all your debugging setup details. This debugging configuration information is used when you debug your project.

Listing 5-16. The launch.json file contents

```
"version": "0.2.0",
"configurations": [
    {
        "name": ".NET Core Launch (console)",
        "type": "coreclr",
        "request": "launch",
        "preLaunchTask": "build",
        "program": "${workspaceFolder}/bin/Debug/netcoreapp3.0/
        aspnetmvc.dll",
        "args": [],
        "cwd": "${workspaceFolder}",
        "stopAtEntry": false,
        "console": "internalConsole"
    },
```

```
{
    "name": ".NET Core Launch (web)",
    "type": "coreclr",
    "request": "launch",
    "preLaunchTask": "build",
    // If you have changed target frameworks, make sure to update
    the program path.
    "program": "${workspaceFolder}/bin/Debug/netcoreapp3.0/
    aspnetmvc.dll",
    "args": [],
    "cwd": "${workspaceFolder}",
    "stopAtEntry": false,
    "internalConsoleOptions": "openOnSessionStart",
    "launchBrowser": {
        "enabled": true,
        "args": "${auto-detect-url}",
        "windows": {
            "command": "cmd.exe",
            "args": "/C start ${auto-detect-url}"
        },
        "osx": {
            "command": "open"
        },
        "linux": {
            "command": "xdg-open"
        }
    },
    "env": {
        "ASPNETCORE_ENVIRONMENT": "Development"
    },
    "sourceFileMap": {
        "/Views": "${workspaceFolder}/Views"
    }
},
{
```

```
            "name": ".NET Core Attach",
            "type": "coreclr",
            "request": "attach",
            "processId": "${command:pickProcess}"
        }
    ,]
}
```

The next file we see is the tasks.json file. This runs the build task on your ASP.NET Core MVC project. It can contain several other tasks, but for now this is all we need.

Listing 5-17. The tasks.json file contents

```
{
    "version": "2.0.0",
    "tasks": [
        {
            "label": "build",
            "command": "dotnet build",
            "type": "shell",
            "group": "build",
            "presentation": {
                "reveal": "silent"
            },
            "problemMatcher": "$msCompile"
        }
    ]
}
```

Next, expand the *Views* ➤ *Home* folder and open the *Index.cshtml* file. Place a breakpoint on line 4 as can be seen in Figure 5-20 by clicking the margin.

```
≡ Index.cshtml  ●
 1   @{
 2       ViewData["Title"] = "Home Page";
 3       var longAgoDate = DateTime.Today.AddYears(-100);
●◄─4       var longDayOfWeek = longAgoDate.DayOfWeek;
 5   }
 6
 7   <div class="text-center">                    Breakpoint
 8       <h1 class="display-4">Welcome</h1>
 9       <h2 class="display-4">100 Years ago was
10           @longDayOfWeek
11           , @longAgoDate.ToString("MMMM dd, yyyy")
12       </h2>
13   </div>
```

Figure 5-20. *Placing a breakpoint*

We now need to hold down *Ctrl+Shift+D* to bring up the debugging pane as seen in Figure 5-21. First off you will notice that you have access to the familiar variables, Watch and Call Stack. You will also see the breakpoints group with the currently set breakpoint indicated on the *Index.cshtml* file.

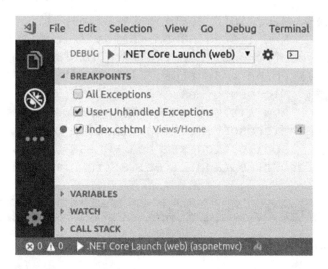

Figure 5-21. *The debugging pane*

From the Debug combobox, select *.NET Core Launch (web)* and click the green play button (Figure 5-22).

Figure 5-22. *Debug started*

The project will go through a build, and if this is successful, the debug bar will be displayed enabled at the top of the Visual Studio Code IDE window. Now you want to open up the *Debug Console*. You can do this via the *View ➤ Debug Console* menu or by holding down *Ctrl+Shift+Y*. You will see the familiar output we saw earlier and you will notice that it states that the Microsoft.Hosting.Lifetime web host is listening on localhost (Figure 5-23).

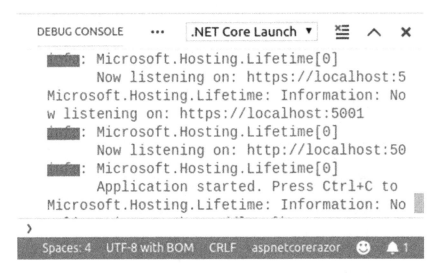

Figure 5-23. *Debug Console*

Swing back to your browser (I'm using Firefox) and enter the URL specified in the Debug Console.

```
      Help                Index.cshtml - aspnetmvc - Visual Studio Code [Superuser]

     1   @{
     2       ViewData["Title"] = "Home Page";
     3       var longAgoDate = DateTime.Today.AddYears(-100);
  •  4       var longDayOfWeek = longAgoDate.DayOfWeek;
     5   }
     6
     7   <div class="text-center">
     8       <h1 class="display-4">Welcome</h1>
     9       <h2 class="display-4">100 Years ago was
    10           @longDayOfWeek
    11           , @longAgoDate.ToString("MMMM dd, yyyy")
    12       </h2>
    13   </div>
```

Figure 5-24. *Breakpoint hit*

When your web page loads, your breakpoint will be hit as shown in Figure 5-24. You are now able to step through your code, view variables, use the watch window, and perform all the normal debugging task as you would normally. You can also inspect your variables by hovering over the variable in the editor as you step through your lines of code.

Wrapping Up

We have a wealth of information online in the form of Microsoft Documentation (https://docs.microsoft.com) that have just what you are looking for. I hope at least this chapter piqued your interest in what is available in .NET Core 3.0. As the framework evolves, we will see a lot more features included with each release.

This chapter had a look at creating .NET Core applications. We saw that we can now create a Windows desktop application on .NET Core, but that these are only supported on Windows.

Then we had a look at what some of the more interesting new features are in .NET Core 3.0. We saw that we have support for C# 8, fast built-in JSON support, and cryptography.

We saw that we can install .NET Core 3.0 on Linux using Snap. Staying with Linux, we created an ASP.NET Core MVC application and ran it on Linux. Using Visual Studio Code, we saw that it was possible to edit our project files, and lastly, we saw that we were able to debug our applications on Linux using Visual Studio Code.

If you enjoy the flexibility of Visual Studio Code, stay tuned. In the next chapter, we are going to take a tour through Visual Studio 2019 and have a look at what is new in the upcoming release of this world-class IDE. Are you excited? I know I am.

CHAPTER 6

Being More Productive in Visual Studio

Visual Studio has come a really long way since its initial release as Visual Studio 97 over 20 years ago. Personally, I have been working with the IDE since 2003 and have loved seeing it evolve into what it is today. The problem, though, is that developers get so bogged down in the everydayness of writing code that they tend to miss new features and productivity improvements with newer versions.

In part, I think that this is because developers are focused on getting the job done. We do live and work in a fast-paced, deadline-oriented industry. It is therefore easy to brush over getting to know the new release better, because you need to get the job done. I have often heard developers say "I didn't know you could do that!".

In fact, many developers are quite focused on learning the new features of C# (for example), and rightly so. Let's for a moment (or a chapter) pause at the foot of our old friend, the trusty IDE, that makes it all possible.

This chapter will take a look at what the new release (currently in Preview) offers us in terms of productivity improvements and features.

At the time of writing this chapter, Visual Studio 2019 was in Preview 3. It might change slightly before the final release, but most of the things discussed in this chapter should remain the same.

I will also have a look at some existing features and goodies that can make your life easier in your day-to-day development efforts. We will be looking at

- New features in Visual Studio 2019

- Visual Studio Live Share

© Dirk Strauss 2019
D. Strauss, *Exploring Advanced Features in C#*, https://doi.org/10.1007/978-1-4842-4856-0_6

- Refactorings and code fixes

- Enable JavaScript debugging in ASP.NET projects

- Exporting your editor settings

- Visual Studio IntelliCode using AI

- General Visual Studio Tips

It's about to get a lot more exciting, so let's get going with Visual Studio 2019.

New Features in Visual Studio 2019

Visual Studio 2019 brings what matters most to developers in a more condensed and focused way by providing a fresh perspective on the UI.

UI Improvements

The first thing you will probably notice about Visual Studio 2019 is the new start screen as seen in Figure 6-1.

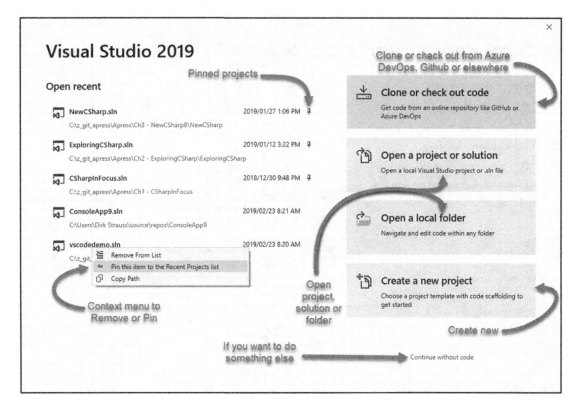

Figure 6-1. *Visual Studio 2019 start menu*

Microsoft has brought the most often used tasks developers perform front and center with its overhauled start menu. It's really easy to get going with what matters most in Visual Studio, and that is writing code.

Speaking of writing code, the new project dialog also provides improvements over the way you select project templates. Apart from it allowing you to select from a list of recent project types, you can filter the project templates by selecting from dropdown menus that filter by Language, Platform, or Project type as can be seen in Figure 6-2.

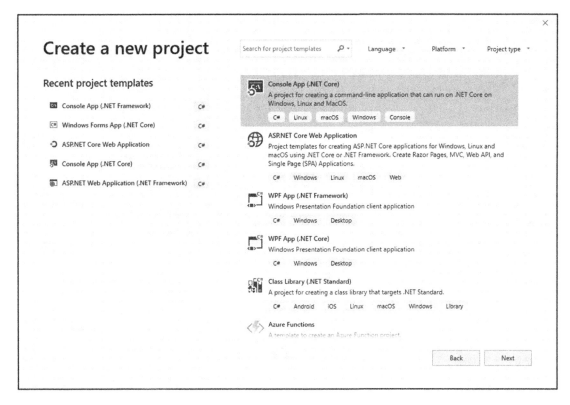

Figure 6-2. *The new project dialog*

This allows you to search for and select project templates quickly and get started writing code. Moving on to the IDE itself, Visual Studio 2019 minimizes clutter much more than in Visual Studio 2017, simply by minimizing the chrome and compressing the menu. This has the effect of giving you more space to write code in. Compare the IDE chrome and menu bar in Visual Studio 2017 with that in Visual Studio 2019.

Figure 6-3 is what we are currently used to seeing in Visual Studio 2017.

Figure 6-3. *Visual Studio 2017*

Figure 6-4 shows the changes in Visual Studio 2019. You will notice that the icon has changed and that the Visual Studio 2019 IDE looks tighter.

Figure 6-4. *Visual Studio 2019*

In fact, notice how the image of Visual Studio 2017 doesn't include the *Start* button, while the image of Visual Studio 2019 does. This is due in part to the shortening of the Solution Configurations and Solutions Platforms dropdown menus.

Search Improvements

In Visual Studio 2019, you can click the search bar (Figure 6-5) in the menu or hold down Ctrl+Q to jump your cursor from the code editor to the search textbox.

Figure 6-5. *Visual Studio 2019 search bar*

This allows you to start typing immediately and search for what you need as seen in Figure 6-6.

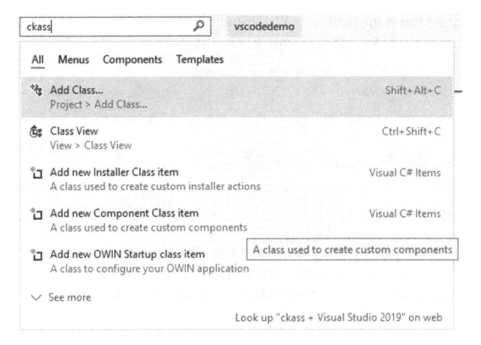

Figure 6-6. *Search results in Visual Studio 2019*

Search results are displayed quickly, which gives the IDE a snappier feel (especially if you are focused on your code). You will notice that I mistyped the search term *class*, but Visual Studio 2019 still returned relevant results for me using fuzzy search.

The search results include the menu path to whatever it is that you are looking for. Using Visual Studio search, however, gives you a shortcut into these menus so you can essentially keep your hands on your keyboard. Another important point to note is that now you can create new items directly from the Visual Studio 2019 search results. In the preceding example, you can see that I can add a new class right from within my search results.

Lastly, if you don't see the result that you are looking for, you can click the link at the bottom of the search results to search on the web.

These improvements to search make Visual Studio 2019 easier to navigate and find your way around a really feature-rich IDE. Quickly, find *C# Interactive*! Go!

Cleaning Up Your Code

Visual Studio 2019 gives you a lot of control over your code and how that code is to be formatted. A great way to do this is through code cleanup.

Visual Studio allows you to configure your Code Cleanup, so let's do this. Use the search bar to look for the word *cleanup* as can be seen in Figure 6-7.

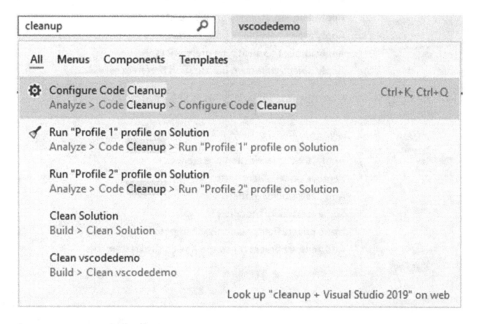

Figure 6-7. *Searching for Code Cleanup config screen*

You will see that the search results include *Configure Code Cleanup*. You can also hold down Ctrl+K, Ctrl+Q to open the configuration screen.

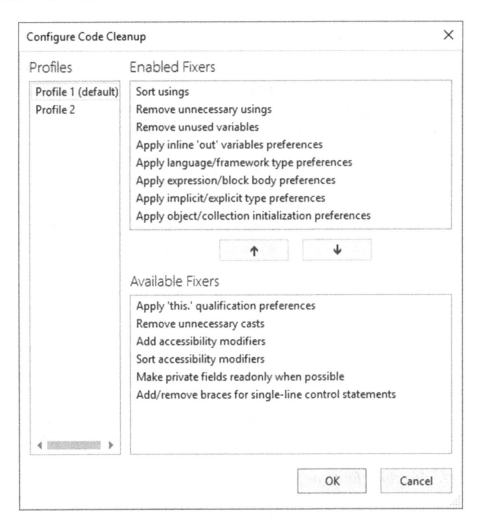

Figure 6-8. *Configure Code Cleanup*

The configuration screen in Figure 6-8 allows you to enable fixers that you want to apply in your code. Notice that I have added *Apply inline 'out' variables preferences* to my *Enabled Fixers* list. You can also apply these preferences to another profile.

Wouldn't it be nice if we could add/rename profiles? Hint hint Visual Studio team.

Back in my code editor, you will see that I can click a little brush icon (Figure 6-9) to perform a code cleanup.

```
50
                1 reference | 0 changes | 0 authors, 0 changes
51      ⊟  public static void NotSuchNiceCode()
52         {
53             int iValue = 5;
54             ZeroValue(out iValue);
55             WriteLine($"The variable changed to: {iValue}");
56         }
57
                1 reference | 0 changes | 0 authors, 0 changes
58      ⊟  public static void ZeroValue(out int iValue)
59         {
60             iValue = 0;
61         }
62
```

100 % ▾   ✓ No issues found   ✐ ▾   ◄

Error List

□ Ln 47   Col 31   Ch 31   INS

Figure 6-9. *Code before Code Cleanup*

I can also click the down arrow to see more options such as running the code cleanup associated to the specific profile as seen in Figure 6-10. I can also access the Code Cleanup Configuration from here too.

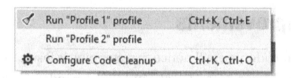

✐	Run "Profile 1" profile	Ctrl+K, Ctrl+E
	Run "Profile 2" profile	
⚙	Configure Code Cleanup	Ctrl+K, Ctrl+Q

Figure 6-10. *Run Code Cleanup*

For now, I just want to apply the inline 'out' variables preferences. Hit the brush icon or hold down *Ctrl+K, Ctrl+E* and your code will be cleaned according to your Code Cleanup preferences. You can see the results in Figure 6-11.

```
45
     1 reference | 0 changes | 0 authors, 0 changes
46  ⊟  public static void NotSuchNiceCode()
47     {
48         ZeroValue(out int iValue);
49         WriteLine($"The variable changed to: {iValue}");
50     }
51

     1 reference | 0 changes | 0 authors, 0 changes
52  ⊟  public static void ZeroValue(out int iValue)
53     {
54         iValue = 0;
55     }
56
57
```

100 % ▾   ✅ No issues found   🖌 ▾   ◀

Error List

▢ Ready   Ln 40   Col 18   Ch 18

Figure 6-11. *Code cleaned up*

Apart from configuring the Code Cleanup profile, I had to do nothing at all in order to improve the quality of my code. This is the incredible power and value add of the new Visual Studio 2019.

Debugging Improvements

When you debug your code, you will notice that stepping is faster. You will also notice that you can now search your *Autos*, *Locals*, and *Watch* windows via an included search bar (Figure 6-12).

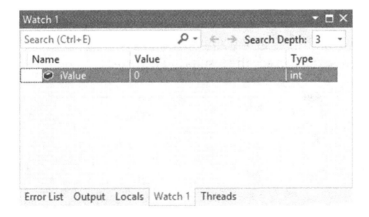

Figure 6-12. *Watch window includes search functionality*

This is really convenient, especially if you have many items in your window that you need to look through. You will also see that you have a default search depth which is set to 3. You can change this, but it means that your results will only drill down your tree three levels deep before the search stops.

Per-Monitor Aware Rendering

If you are using multiple monitors that are configured with different display scale factors, Visual Studio might be slightly blurred or scaled incorrectly. Visual Studio 2019 is laying the foundation that will allow Visual Studio to be a fully per-monitor aware application.

In order to try out the new PMA feature, you will need to have Windows 10 version 1803 (Figure 6-13) or newer, as well as the .NET Framework 4.8 or later installed.

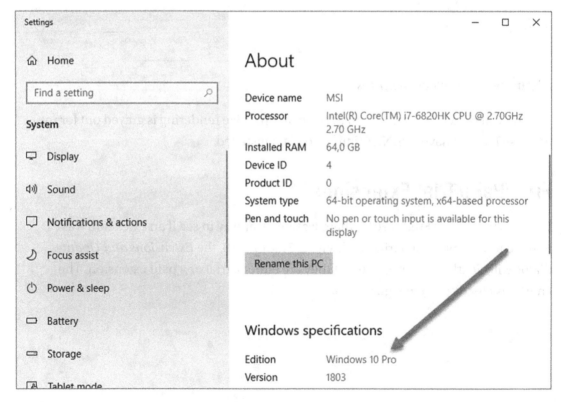

Figure 6-13. *Windows 10 requirements*

You can enable preview features by going to Tools ➤ Options and clicking Environment ➤ Preview Features as can be seen in Figure 6-14.

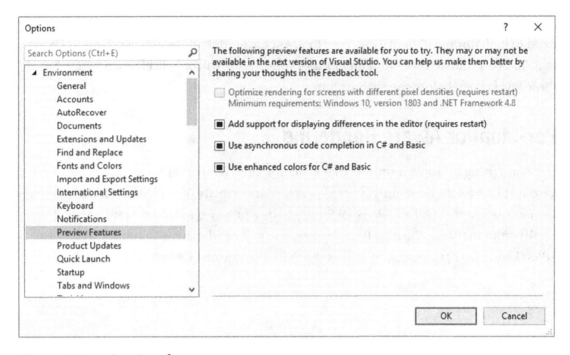

Figure 6-14. *Preview features*

You will notice that the option to select to optimize rendering is grayed out for me because I do not have the .NET Framework 4.8 installed.

Free/Paid/Trial Extensions

Previously in Visual Studio 2017, there was no clear way to see if an extension was marked as free, paid, or a trial. With Visual Studio 2019, the *Extensions and Updates* dialog will clearly mark extensions if they are either a trial or a paid extension. The change is clearly seen in Figure 6-15.

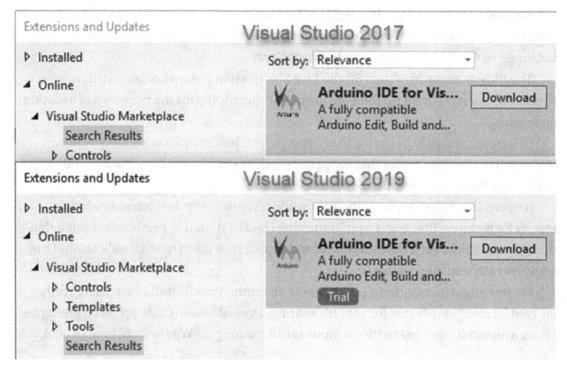

Figure 6-15. *Free/paid/trial extensions*

Free extensions do not have any label, while paid and trial extensions are clearly marked with a blue label.

Visual Studio Live Share

Visual Studio Live Share is a fantastic service that allows you to "phone a friend" essentially. You can share your codebase and its context with a colleague and collaborate with them right from within Visual Studio.

Your colleague can read your code, navigate through it, edit and debug any project you share with them with Visual Studio Live Share. The best of all is that Visual Studio Live Share is included by default in Visual Studio 2019.

To find out more about Visual Studio Live Share, or to download it for Visual Studio Code or Visual Studio 2017, go to `https://visualstudio.microsoft.com/ services/live-share/`

Yes, you heard that right. It's available for Visual Studio Code. The service works perfectly well between two developers, irrespective of project type, programming language, or OS that you happen to be working on.

The huge bonus with Visual Studio Live Share is that it does not require developers to pull down a repo or set up their environment specifically for the purposes of assisting colleagues.

In the past, the pain of having to set up a project just to assist another developer was compounded by the fact that the person assisting might not have the dependencies needed for the project installed.

It opens the doors for participating in code reviews easily. Just imagine what it means for lecturers that teach a programming class to students. Personally, I think that the lecturers might get a little less exercise now that they don't have to walk around the computer lab, assisting students.

So, you might be wondering exactly how awesome Visual Studio Live Share really is? Well let me quantify that for you. It's sharing a Visual Studio Code project running on Linux with a colleague using Visual Studio 2019 running on Windows 10 kind of cool.

Sharing Your Code

My friend Jason Williams is living in New York. He has just started learning the ropes of programming and wants to start writing ASP.NET Core MVC applications. He is having a bit of trouble with the Razor and needs my help to show him how to add a C# variable into the HTML.

He uses Visual Studio Code as his IDE and has already set up his project and has added some code. Let's see how we can use Visual Studio Live Share to solve his problem.

Inside Visual Studio Code, Jason has installed the VS Live Share extension and enabled it.

In this example, Jason is already logged in to Live Share via his GitHub account. Sometimes, Live Share doesn't recognize the browser sign in within VS Code. I will show you in the section after this how to sign in via a user code if you're having trouble.

Jason clicks the Live Share icon (step 1) to open the Live Share panel. He then clicks *Start collaboration session* under the *Session Details* section (Figure 6-16).

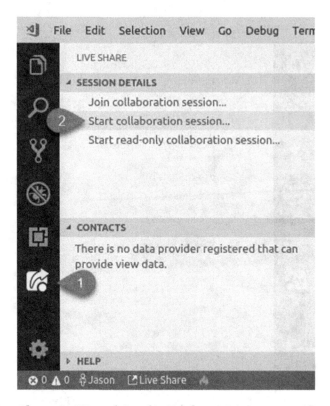

Figure 6-16. *Live Share in Visual Studio Code on Linux*

From Figure 6-17, you can see that the session details now change to show

- Participants

- Shared Servers

- Shared Terminals

I haven't joined the session yet because Jason needs to send me the invitation link.

Figure 6-17. *Live Share session started*

In Visual Studio Code, a notification pops up (Figure 6-18) telling Jason that the invitation link has been copied to the clipboard.

Figure 6-18. *Notification with invitation link*

This is the link he sends to me via IM or email. Whatever works best.

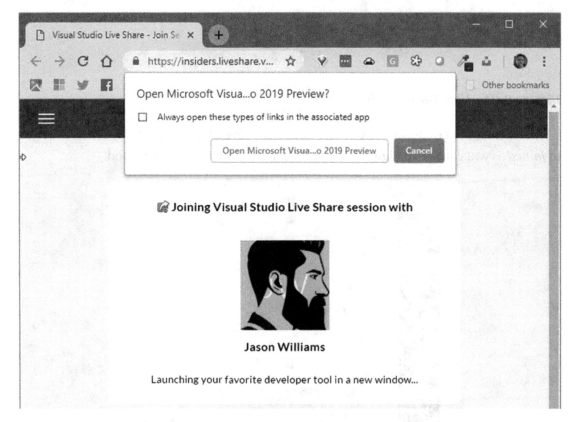

Figure 6-19. *Invitation link pasted into my browser on Windows*

In my office, I have just sat down to start my day when a message with the invitation link from Jason comes through on Skype (yes, Jason is up very late in NYC). I paste the link into my browser (Figure 6-19) and get the option to open the session in Visual Studio 2019.

Figure 6-20. *Joining the Live Share session in Visual Studio 2019*

A new instance of Visual Studio 2019 is launched and displays a *Joining* status as seen in Figure 6-20, with a download cloud icon.

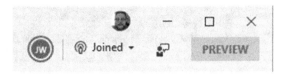

Figure 6-21. *Live Share session joined*

As soon as I have successfully connected to the Live Share session, my status changes to *Joined* as you can see in Figure 6-21, and I can see Jason's icon displayed.

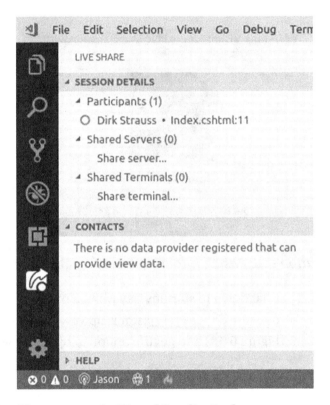

Figure 6-22. *Live Share status in Visual Studio Code*

Back on Jason's Linux machine (Figure 6-22), he can see that I am currently joined in on the session and looking at the *Index.cshtml* file on line 11.

```
Index.cshtml  ⇆ ✕
                                                      ▾
     1     ⊟@{
     2              ViewData["Title"] = "Home Page";
     3              var dtDate = DateTime.Now.Add Jason Williams
     4              var today = dtDate.DayOfWeek;
     5         }
     6
     7     ⊟<div class="text-center">
     8              <h1 class="display-4">Welcome</h1>
     9
    10       </div>
    11
```

Figure 6-23. *Identifying Jason's cursor in Visual Studio 2019*

Back on my Windows PC (Figure 6-23), I can see that Jason currently has his cursor at the end of line 4 of the code, as a label with his name pops up momentarily.

```
≡ Index.cshtml  ✕
     1     @{
     2             ViewData["Title"] = "Home Page";
     3             var dtDate = DateTime.Now.AddDays(-100);
     4             var today = dtDate.DayOfWeek;
     5     }
     6
     7     <div class="text-center">             Dirk Strauss
     8             <h1 class="display-4">Welcome</h1>
     9
    10     </div>
    11
```

Figure 6-24. *Identifying Dirk's cursor in Visual Studio Code*

In Jason's Visual Studio Code, he can see that I have selected the text *Welcome*, by the label with my name that momentarily pops up (Figure 6-24). Throughout the session, labels with our names will display momentarily in each other's code editors as we navigate around the code. There will always be a cursor though, identifying the placement of our cursors to each other.

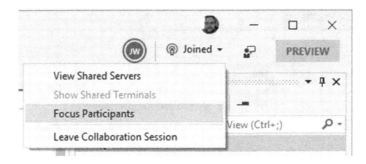

Figure 6-25. *Sending a Focus request to participants*

If I need to focus Jason's attention to a particular line of code, I can send him a Focus notification (Figure 6-25).

```
Index.cshtml*   ⊅ ✕

 1    @{
 2            ViewData["Title"] = "Home Page";
 3            var dtDate = DateTime.Now.AddDays(-100);
 4            var today = dtDate.DayOfWeek;
 5        }
 6
 7    <div class="text-center">
 8            <h1 class="display-4">Welcome to @today</h1>
 9    </div>
10
```

Figure 6-26. *Editing Jason's code in Visual Studio 2019*

The problem Jason had was inserting a variable into the HTML of his page. In my session, on Visual Studio 2019, I modify his code as can be seen in Figure 6-26 and add the today variable to the H1 tag.

Notice that the Index.cshtml file is marked as unsaved in Visual Studio 2019.

```
≡ Index.cshtml ●
 1   @{
 2       ViewData["Title"] = "Home Page";
 3       var dtDate = DateTime.Now.AddDays(-100);
 4       var today = dtDate.DayOfWeek;
 5   }
 6
 7   <div class="text-center">                    Dirk Strauss
 8       <h1 class="display-4">Welcome to @today</h1>
 9   </div>
10
```

Figure 6-27. *Jason's code edited in Visual Studio Code*

Jason now immediately sees the code change I made (Figure 6-27) and understands that the way to add a variable into his HTML is to prefix the variable with the @ sign. Jason is currently 7 hours behind me. He is burning the midnight oil and I am able to assist him quickly and efficiently.

- I didn't have to resort to clunky and inefficient screen sharing in Skype, for example.

- I didn't need to download his project from GitHub or have to set it up on my machine in any way.

- I didn't have to set up a Linux VM, nor did I have to install Visual Studio Code.

Jason changed nothing about his environment in order to share his code with me, and I did not have to change anything in my environment in order to help him. Visual Studio Live Share simply just works. It's almost like magic.

When You Are Having Trouble Signing In

There is a lot of documentation surrounding Visual Studio Live Share. Just head on over to https://docs.microsoft.com/en-us/visualstudio/liveshare/ to see what topics are being covered. One of the issues I ran into was signing in. I was running Visual Studio Code on Linux and the browser sign in form didn't pop up when launching Live Share.

Here is a resolution for this issue. Go to the following URL (Figure 6-28) and sign in: https://insiders.liveshare.vsengsaas.visualstudio.com/auth/login

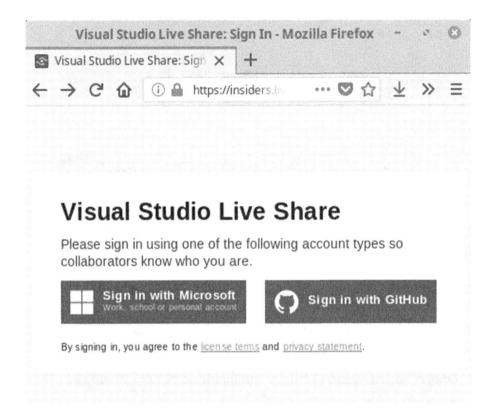

Figure 6-28. *Visual Studio Live Share sign in*

In my case I signed in with my GitHub (Jason's GitHub) account. You can also sign in using a Microsoft account.

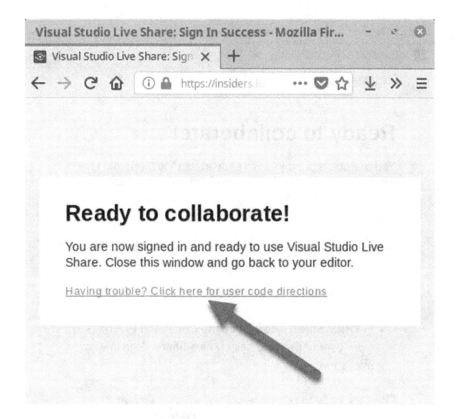

Figure 6-29. *Select user code directions*

Once you see the *Ready to collaborate* screen in Figure 6-29, click the *Having trouble?* link.

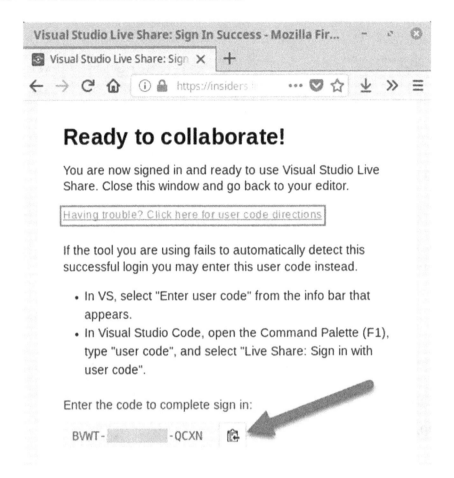

Figure 6-30. *Copy the generated user code*

Copy the user code displayed on the screen (Figure 6-30) and swing back to Visual Studio Code (or Visual Studio if you're having trouble signing in there). Press *F1* in Visual Studio Code to display the *Command Palette* and enter the text "user code". Select the "Live Share: Sign in with user code" option and enter the user code you copied earlier. You should now be able to successfully log in to Live Share.

Sharing Terminals

Another question Jason has is how he can build his project in Visual Studio Code running on Linux.

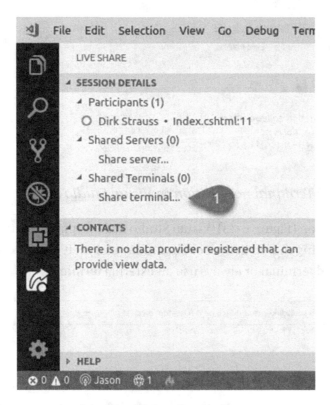

Figure 6-31. *Share terminal in Visual Studio Code*

As it turns out, Jason can easily share his Terminal with me (Figure 6-31) during the Live Share session. Under the *Shared Terminals* section, he simply needs to click the *Share terminal* option.

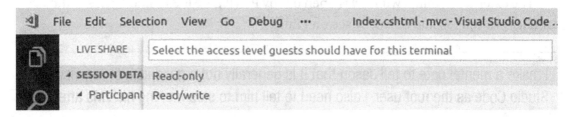

Figure 6-32. *Shared Terminal access level*

He then needs to select what level of access he wants to give me as seen in Figure 6-32. He decides that he needs to give me read/write access.

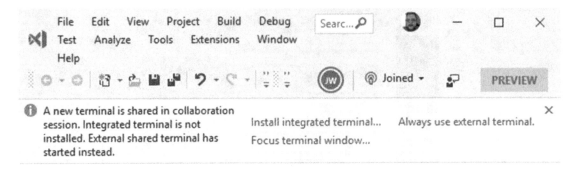

Figure 6-33. *New Terminal notification in Visual Studio 2019*

Back in my session (Figure 6-33), Visual Studio 2019 displays a notification to me that a new terminal is being shared in the collaboration session. It gives me the options to install an integrated terminal or always use an external terminal.

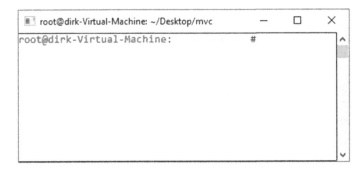

Figure 6-34. *External Terminal window opened in Windows*

The external terminal window is open on my PC (Figure 6-34), and I can see the familiar prompt I would normally see on Linux.

I make a mental note to tell Jason that it is generally not a good idea to run Visual Studio Code as the root user. I also need to tell him to stop naming his VMs after me.

I then enter the command dotnet build in the terminal window on my machine.

Figure 6-35. *Terminal open in Visual Studio Code on Linux*

Back in New York, Jason can see the command as I type it in the Terminal inside Visual Studio Code (Figure 6-35).

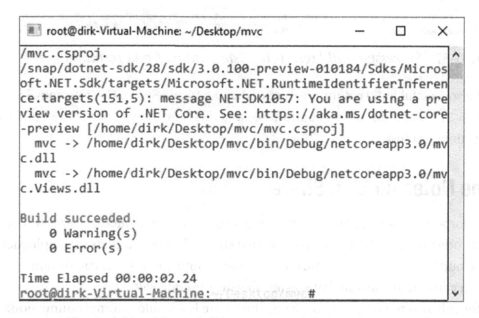

Figure 6-36. *Successful build result from Terminal in Windows*

I then press Enter and the build results are displayed in the Terminal window on my PC (Figure 6-36).

Figure 6-37. *Successful build results in Visual Studio Code Terminal*

The successful build results are mirrored in the Visual Studio Code Terminal window (Figure 6-37), and Jason is now comfortable that he knows how to perform a build using the terminal window.

Some Notes on Live Share

It is important to note that at no point is your code stored on a Microsoft server. The shared code resides only on the machine that shares the code. It is also not uploaded to the cloud in any way. Live Share creates a secure end-to-end encrypted connection between you and the person that you are sharing the code with.

The only real requirement for using Live Share is a stable Internet connection. The secure communication established during a Live Share session is facilitated by an Azure Relay.

At the time of writing this book, Live Share supports five concurrent guests in addition to the developer that initiated the Live Share session. This means that a Live Share session can have six developers in it at any given time. To use Live Share, you need to have Visual Studio 2017 (15.6+), Visual Studio 2019, or Visual Studio Code installed.

Live Share only shares what is needed with collaborators. For example, when you edit a file, only that file's contents are shared. When debugging, debug actions such as stepping and state such as call, stack, and locals are shared.

Visual Studio Live Share is an indispensable tool for developers that are working in a more distributed environment. More and more companies are realizing the benefit of remote developers. Microsoft has now given us the tools to do what we do, irrespective of the distance between colleagues. Give Live Share a try. I know that you will love it as much as I do.

Refactorings and Code Fixes

In this section of the book, we will be looking at some general Visual Studio tips. You can use these in Visual Studio to improve your code and become more productive in your day-to-day coding. As developers, we have the unenviable task of having to work on legacy code. It's never fun. It's almost like playing golf with someone else's clubs. Sometimes it doesn't feel quite right. Let's see how to perfect your swing in Visual Studio.

Convert foreach to LINQ (VS2019 Only)

Did you know that you can refactor a foreach to LINQ in Visual Studio 2019? Kendra Havens, a Program Manager on the .NET team, tweeted this tip a while ago.

As a side note, I would suggest following relevant users on Twitter such as *@gotheap*, *@MadsTorgersen*, *@terrajobst*, and others. You can really pick up some great tips from them as C# and Visual Studio continue to grow.

Let's have a look at a very simple example of a foreach to LINQ. You will see in Figure 6-38 that we want to refactor the foreach section.

```
var lstWidgets =
    new List<string>()
    { "widget1", "widget2", "widget3" };

foreach (var widget in lstWidgets)
{
    if(widget.EndsWith("2"))
    {
        WriteLine($"{widget} exists in the list");
    }
}
```

Figure 6-38. *Simple foreach loop*

This foreach loop can be refactored into LINQ by placing your cursor in front of
the foreach and clicking the lightbulb that appears. You can also hold down *Ctrl+.* or
Alt+Enter and the refactoring menu will be displayed.

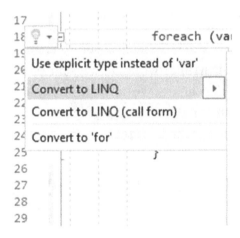

Figure 6-39. *Convert to LINQ*

Clicking *Convert to LINQ* will refactor your code using a query expression as seen in
Figure 6-40.

```
var lstWidgets =
    new List<string>()
    { "widget1", "widget2", "widget3" };

foreach (var widget in from widget in lstWidgets
                       where widget.EndsWith("2")
                       select widget)
{
    WriteLine($"{widget} exists in the list");
}
```

Figure 6-40. *The refactored foreach loop*

If you prefer fluent syntax, you can also select to refactor it by clicking *LINQ (call from)* that refactors the preceding code as seen in Figure 6-41.

```
var lstWidgets =
    new List<string>()
    { "widget1", "widget2", "widget3" };

foreach (var widget in lstWidgets
    .Where(widget => widget.EndsWith("2"))
    .Select(widget => widget))
{
    WriteLine($"{widget} exists in the list");
}
```

Figure 6-41. *LINQ (call from)*

Whichever you prefer, being able to convert a foreach to LINQ is a really nice addition to the code refactoring options in Visual Studio.

Take note that this refactoring will only be available in Visual Studio 2019.

So, which is better to use? Is there even a LINQ fluent vs. query syntax argument to be made here? Let's pause here for a second.

LINQ Fluent vs. Query Syntax

There are basically two ways that you can use code to create LINQ queries. You can use fluent syntax, which uses lambda expressions for the parameters in the query operators. It also feels more modern. The other way is to use a query expression, which feels similar to SQL queries.

The one isn't better than the other. It really depends on your preference and how you are going to be querying. If you use the `let` keyword, do joins, or have multiple `from` clauses, query syntax will probably be the best choice.

The `let` clause allows you to store the result of a sub-expression that you can then use in subsequent clauses.

The following is an example of LINQ using query syntax and the `let` keyword.

Listing 6-1. Query syntax using let

```
var lstStockCode =
    new List<string>()
    { "A100-341", "B101-754", "A100-197", "C201-341", "B102-774", "C101-111",
    "A100-774", "C105-191" };

var classAStockCodes =
    from aclass in lstStockCode
    let a = (aclass.StartsWith("A100") ? (aclass.Replace("A100-", "")) : "0")
    where Convert.ToInt32(a) > 200
    && Convert.ToInt32(a) > 0
    select aclass;

foreach(var cl in classAStockCodes)
{
    WriteLine($"{cl} is a class A stock code in the 200 plus range");
}
```

The code listing illustrates finding all A-class stock codes where the number after the dash is 200 or greater. Using query syntax makes sense here because we had to use the `let` keyword to store the numeric portion of the stock code if the ternary conditional statement evaluated to true. If false, we just returned a zero. We can then pull out the stock codes that conform to our where conditions.

Convert to Interpolated String

The following tip is available in Visual Studio 2017, but I feel that it is worth mentioning, especially since it can simplify code quite a bit when you work with legacy code. Consider the following bit of code.

Listing 6-2. String.Format string

```
string FirstName = "Dirk";
string LastName = "Strauss";
string FullName = string.Format("My name is {0} {1}", FirstName, LastName);
```

The use of `string.Format` is a code that a lot of developers will come across (or even write). Well now there is an option to refactor this code. Clicking the lightbulb (you can press Ctrl+. or Alt+Enter too) will bring up the code refactor menu.

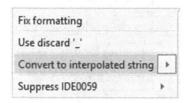

Figure 6-42. *Convert to interpolated string*

This allows you to convert the code to an interpolated string (Figure 6-42). The resulting code is as follows.

Listing 6-3. Formatted to interpolated string

```
string FirstName = "Dirk";
string LastName = "Strauss";
string FullName = $"My name is {FirstName} {LastName}";
```

This style of writing strings that include variables is much more readable, especially if you name your variables well.

Convert Anonymous Type to Class

In C#, the use of anonymous types is used to encapsulate read-only properties into a single object without you having to define a type first. The compiler infers the type of each property. With Visual Studio 2019, you can now convert the anonymous type (Figure 6-43) to a class.

```
var logger = new {
        flag = "start"
        , priority = 10
        , logLevel = "verbose" };
```

Figure 6-43. *The logger anonymous type*

By placing your cursor in front of the new keyword, click the lightbulb, hold down *Ctrl+.* or *Alt+Enter*, and select *Convert to class* (Figure 6-44).

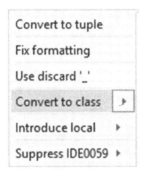

```
Convert to tuple
Fix formatting
Use discard '_'
Convert to class        ▸
Introduce local        ▸
Suppress IDE0059    ▸
```

Figure 6-44. *Select convert to class*

The Rename window pops up and highlights the NewClass name it automatically inserted for you (Figure 6-45).

```
var logger = new NewClass(
        "start"
        , 10
        , "verbose");
```

Figure 6-45. *Renaming the new class name*

Provide a more sensible name for the class you want to create and hit the Enter button.

```
var logger = new LoggerClass(
        "start"
        , 10
        , "verbose");
```

Figure 6-46. *Default class name renamed to LoggerClass*

I called my class LoggerClass (Figure 6-46), and if I scroll down to the bottom of my code file, I will see that Visual Studio 2019 has inserted the new class for me.

Listing 6-4. The generated LoggerClass

```
internal class LoggerClass
{
    public string Flag { get; }
    public int Priority { get; }
    public string LogLevel { get; }

    public LoggerClass(string flag,
                       int priority,
                       string logLevel)
    {
        Flag = flag;
        Priority = priority;
        LogLevel = logLevel;
    }

    public override bool Equals(object obj)
    {
        return obj is LoggerClass other &&
               Flag == other.Flag &&
               Priority == other.Priority &&
               LogLevel == other.LogLevel;
    }
    public override int GetHashCode()
    {
        var hashCode = -1332235279;
        hashCode = hashCode * -1521134295 + System.Collections.Generic.
        EqualityComparer<string>.Default.GetHashCode(Flag);
        hashCode = hashCode * -1521134295 + Priority.GetHashCode();
        hashCode = hashCode * -1521134295 + System.Collections.Generic.
        EqualityComparer<string>.Default.GetHashCode(LogLevel);
        return hashCode;
    }
}
```

Now isn't that just snazzy!

Converting a Local Function to Method

Let's stay with the `LoggerClass` we created from the anonymous type. I am going to add a method called `AddLogEntry` to the class. This method will contain a local function called `DetermineLogLevelPriority` that simply takes the `LogLevel` property value and returns an integer value for it.

```
1 reference | 0 changes | 0 authors, 0 changes
public void AddLogEntry()       Local Function
{
    int DetermineLogLevelPriority()
    {
        return LogLevel.ToLower() switch
        {
            "verbose"   => 10,
            "info"      => 5,
            "minimal"   => 1,
            _           => 0
        };
    }                      switch expression

    int iLogLevel = DetermineLogLevelPriority();
    Log(iLogLevel, Priority, Flag);
}
```

Figure 6-47.   *The DetermineLogLevelPriority local function*

The local function uses a switch to return an integer value for the `LogLevel` value passed to the class (Figure 6-47).

If the `switch` statement looks a little funny to you, have a look at switch expressions in Chapter 3 of this book. Switch expressions are a new language feature of C# 8.

Personally, I really like local functions. Let's for a minute assume that the `DetermineLogLevelPriority` method now no longer makes sense to use as a local function. This could be as a result of needing the logic that the local function provides, somewhere else in the class. In Visual Studio 2019, we can convert the local function to a method by placing our cursor in front of the local function name and hold down *Ctrl+.* or *Alt+Enter* and select *Convert to method* option (Figure 6-48).

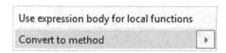

Figure 6-48. *Convert to method*

Visual Studio refactors your local function to a method that you can now call from anywhere in your class.

```
1 reference | 0 changes | 0 authors, 0 changes
public void AddLogEntry()
{
                    Local function to method
    int iLogLevel = DetermineLogLevelPriority();
    Log(iLogLevel, Priority, Flag);
}

1 reference | 0 changes | 0 authors, 0 changes
private int DetermineLogLevelPriority()
{
    return LogLevel.ToLower() switch
    {
        "verbose"   => 10,
        "info"      => 5,
        "minimal"   => 1,
        _           => 0
    };
}
```

Figure 6-49. *Local function converted to a method*

Code refactoring such as this saves you a lot of time rewriting code and copying and pasting code around to change things up.

Enable JavaScript Debugging in ASP.NET Projects

If you create a new browser config in the *Browse With* menu for an ASP.NET project, Visual Studio 2019 will enable JavaScript debugging for your project when you launch your debug session. Go ahead and create a new ASP.NET MVC application.

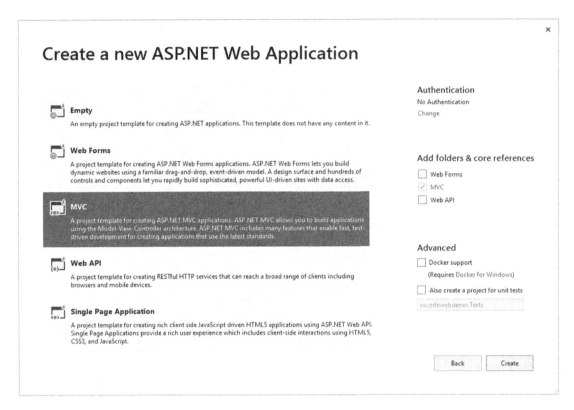

Figure 6-50. *New ASP.NET Web Application dialog*

You will see from Figure 6-50 that this dialog has also had a nice overhaul. We're going to stick with the default settings here and just click the *Create* button. When your project is created, right-click the *Index.cshtml* file in the *Home* folder under *Views* and select Browse With.

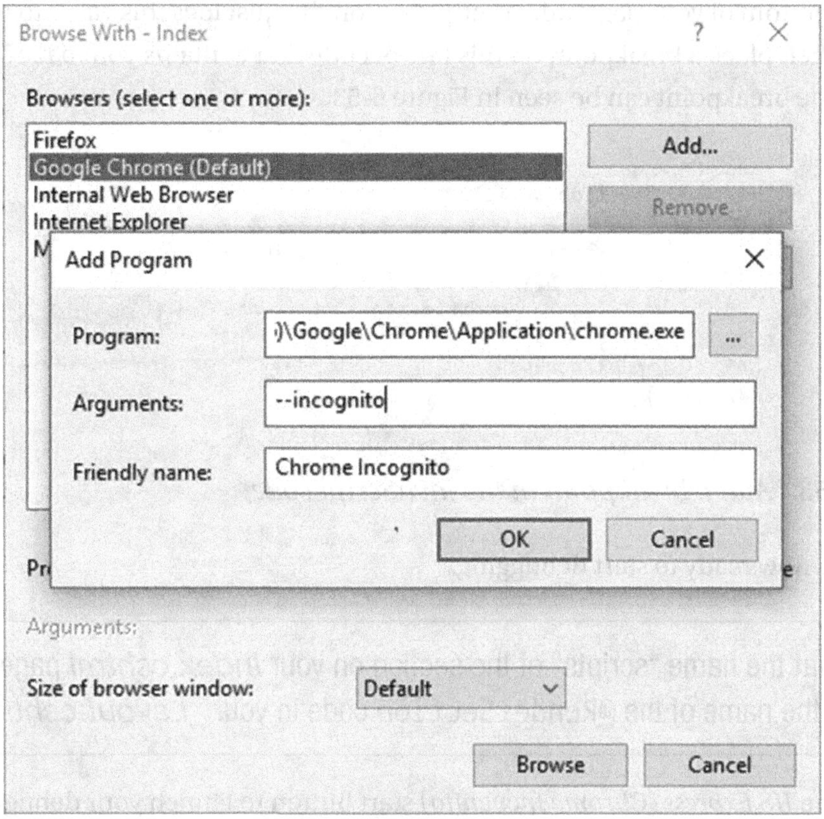

Figure 6-51. *Add new Browse With setting*

Select the path to Google Chrome and pass the `--incognito` argument as seen in Figure 6-51. Then give it a friendly name and click OK. Set Chrome Incognito as your default and then cancel out of the Browse With screen.

Double-click the *Index.cshtml* page and view the code. Add a variable to hold the current date and time value (Figure 6-52).

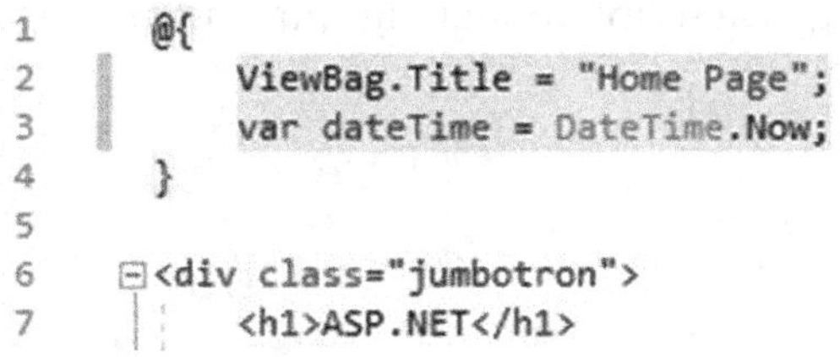

```
1    @{
2        ViewBag.Title = "Home Page";
3        var dateTime = DateTime.Now;
4    }
5
6    <div class="jumbotron">
7        <h1>ASP.NET</h1>
```

Figure 6-52. *Add a variable for today's date*

At the bottom of your page, add a script section that just logs this value to the console window. Then place a breakpoint on this line of code that contains your `dateTime` variable. The breakpoint can be seen in Figure 6-53.

```
33
34       @section scripts
35       {
36  ⊟        <script type="text/javascript">
37  ⊟            $(function() {
38                   console.log( "It is now " + @dateTime );
39               });
40           </script>
41       }
```

Figure 6-53. *Add a breakpoint in the JavaScript code*

You are now ready to start debugging.

Ensure that the name "scripts" of the section on your *Index.cshtml* page matches the name of the @`RenderSection` code in your *_Layout.cshtml* file.

Click the *IIS Express (Chrome Incognito)* start button to launch your debug session (Figure 6-54).

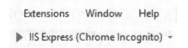

Figure 6-54. *Debug with Chrome Incognito*

Visual Studio now detects that I have added a breakpoint to some JavaScript code and displays the following JavaScript debugging warning message as seen in Figure 6-55.

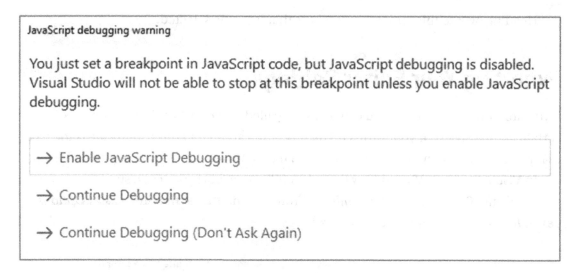

Figure 6-55. *JavaScript debugging warning*

If you select *Enable JavaScript Debugging* from here, Visual Studio sets this option on for you in *Tools, Options, Debugging, General, Enable JavaScript debugging for ASP.NET (Chrome, Edge and IE)* as seen in Figure 6-56.

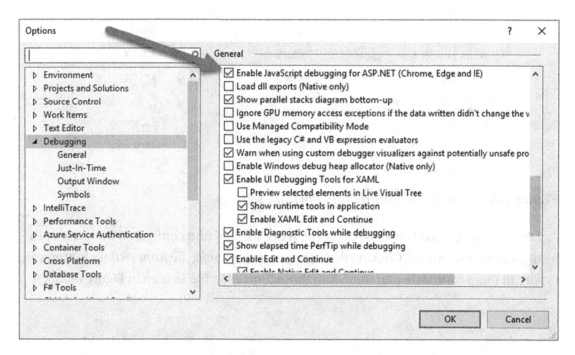

Figure 6-56. *JavaScript debugging enabled in Options*

Heading over to this option, you will see that it is now selected.

Exporting Your Editor Settings

If you are working in a team, you can use a file called an *EditorConfig* file to enforce certain coding styles for your project. The nice thing about an *EditorConfig* file is the fact that you can check it in to source control and have it travel with each new pull of the repo.

In Visual Studio 2019, you now have the ability to export your code style settings, as seen in Figure 6-57, to an *EditorConfig* file. You can find this option in *Tools* ➤ *Options* ➤ *Text Editor* ➤ *C#* ➤ *Code Style* ➤ *General*.

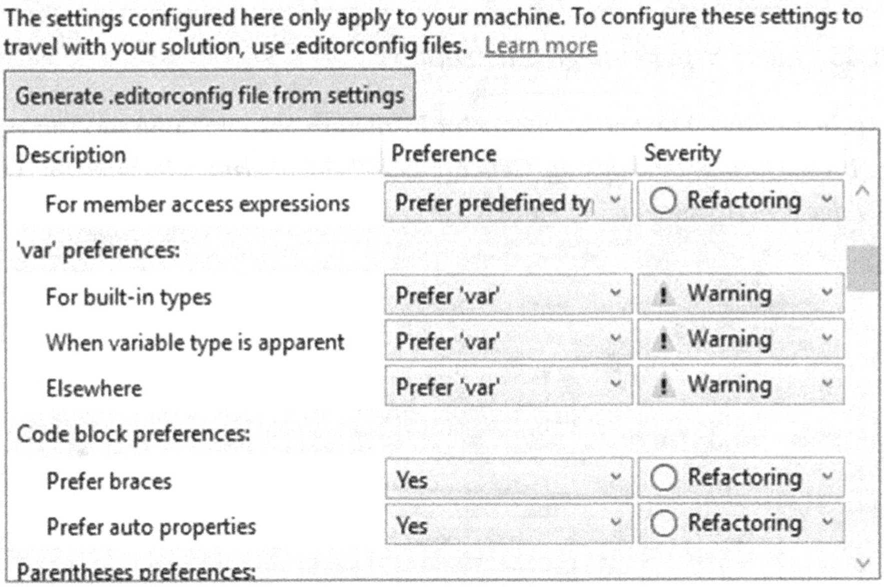

Figure 6-57. *Generate .editorconfig file from settings*

You will notice that I specified my preference for 'var' and configured the severity to be displayed as warnings. Clicking the *Generate .editorconfig file from settings* button will export all these code style preferences to the *.editorconfig* file as seen in Figure 6-58.

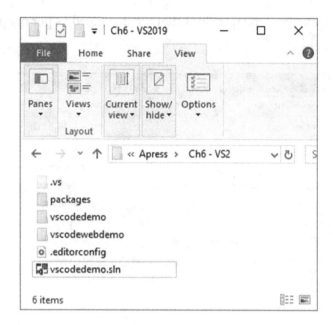

Figure 6-58. *Generated .editorconfig file*

The file is now determining the style of your code, because the file takes precedence over global Visual Studio text editor settings. You can still set your own style preferences in the Visual Studio *Options* dialog, but those style preferences will only be applied in a project that does not contain an *.editorconfig* file or where the style in the *.editorconfig* file does not supersede the style preference you have set.

Figure 6-59. *Document health indicator*

With the *.editorconfig* file applied to my project, I immediately see some warnings according to the preferences I have set (Figure 6-59). Other developers working on the same project will also see these warnings.

If I look at my code, I will see some squiggly lines appear (Figure 6-60) under the explicit types.

```
string FirstName = "Dirk";
string LastName = "Strauss";
string FullName = $"My name is {FirstName} {LastName}";
```

Figure 6-60. *Squiggly lines appear*

Figure 6-61 also shows some warnings that are displayed as per my preference in the
.*editorconfig* file.

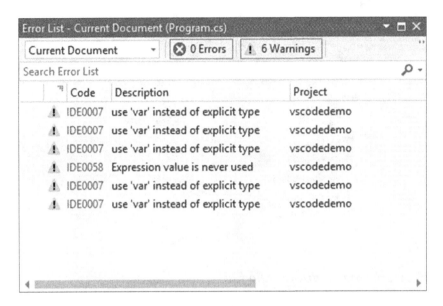

Figure 6-61. *Warnings displayed for explicit types*

Opening the .editorconfig file, I can see the style preferences I had set and exported
(Figure 6-62).

```
.editorconfig ⊸ ✕
    64    # var preferences
    65    csharp_style_var_elsewhere = true:warning
    66    csharp_style_var_for_built_in_types = true:warning
    67    csharp_style_var_when_type_is_apparent = true:warning
    68
```

Figure 6-62. *The .editorconfig file*

Another thing to note is that Visual Studio will clearly notify you via the status bar
that it is using an .*editorconfig* file for user preferences (Figure 6-63).

Figure 6-63. *Status showing .editorconfig is in use*

Being able to export your code style preferences allows you and your team to easily share code style preferences and maintain a consistent coding style across several or all of your projects.

Visual Studio IntelliCode Using AI

In 2018 during Build, Microsoft announced the AI-powered Visual Studio IntelliCode. It is aimed at improving the productivity of developers by providing recommendations on contextual code completion, inferring style rules, and code formatting. It is available for Visual Studio 2017, Visual Studio 2019, and Visual Studio Code as an optional extension as seen in Figure 6-64.

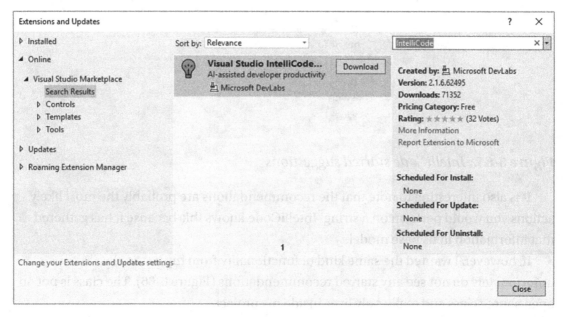

Figure 6-64. *Visual Studio IntelliCode extension*

IntelliCode's recommendations have been based off of learning patterns from thousands of open source repos. With the extension installed in Visual Studio, you will see that IntelliCode's base model stars some recommendations for IntelliSense. This is different from the normal alphabetical order it used to be displayed as.

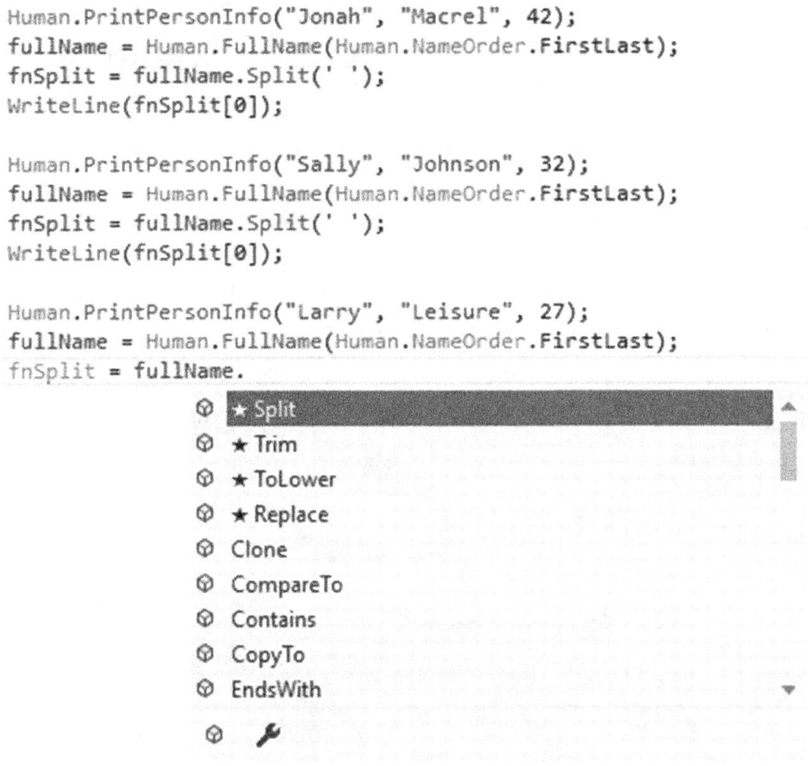
Human.PrintPersonInfo("Jonah", "Macrel", 42);
fullName = Human.FullName(Human.NameOrder.FirstLast);
fnSplit = fullName.Split(' ');
WriteLine(fnSplit[0]);
Human.PrintPersonInfo("Sally", "Johnson", 32);
fullName = Human.FullName(Human.NameOrder.FirstLast);
fnSplit = fullName.Split(' ');
WriteLine(fnSplit[0]);
Human.PrintPersonInfo("Larry", "Leisure", 27);
fullName = Human.FullName(Human.NameOrder.FirstLast);
fnSplit = fullName.
★ Split
★ Trim
★ ToLower
★ Replace
Clone
CompareTo
Contains
CopyTo
EndsWith

Figure 6-65. *IntelliCode starred suggestions*

It is also interesting to note that the recommendations are probably the most likely actions you would perform on a string. IntelliCode knows this because it has gathered that information in its base model.

If, however, I wanted the same kind of functionality from my `Human` class, I unfortunately do not see any starred recommendations (Figure 6-66). The class is not an open source class and really only lives inside my project.

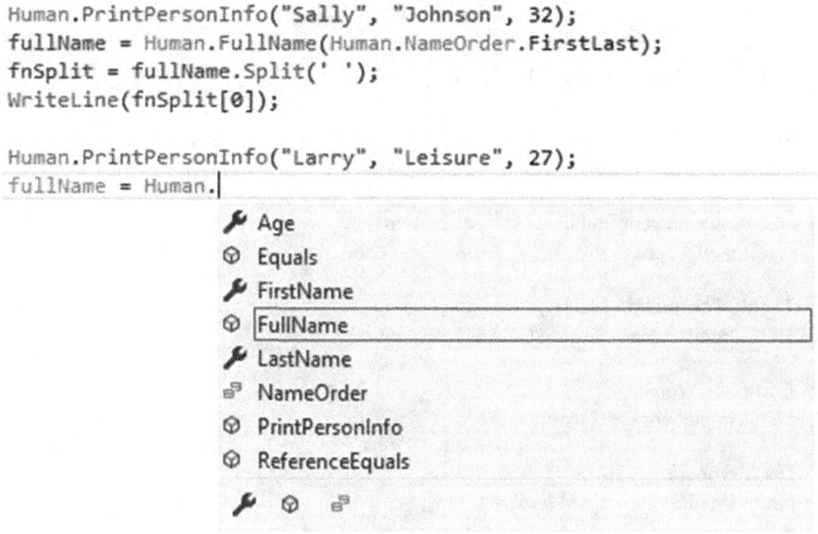

```
Human.PrintPersonInfo("Sally", "Johnson", 32);
fullName = Human.FullName(Human.NameOrder.FirstLast);
fnSplit = fullName.Split(' ');
WriteLine(fnSplit[0]);

Human.PrintPersonInfo("Larry", "Leisure", 27);
fullName = Human.
```

- 🔧 Age
- ⊕ Equals
- 🔧 FirstName
- ⊕ FullName
- 🔧 LastName
- ⬛ NameOrder
- ⊕ PrintPersonInfo
- ⊕ ReferenceEquals

🔧 ⊕ ⬛

Figure 6-66. *No starred suggestions on Human class*

This is because IntelliCode has not built up any custom models to use to provide recommendations. In order to build these custom models, you need to open your IntelliCode window and train it on your code base. It is currently under *View ➤ Other Windows ➤ IntelliCode,* but I expect this to change in upcoming releases of Visual Studio 2019. The easiest way to find the IntelliCode window is to probably use the excellent search capabilities in Visual Studio 2019.

Hit *Ctrl+Q* and start typing (Figure 6-67). Then click the first result to open the IntelliCode window.

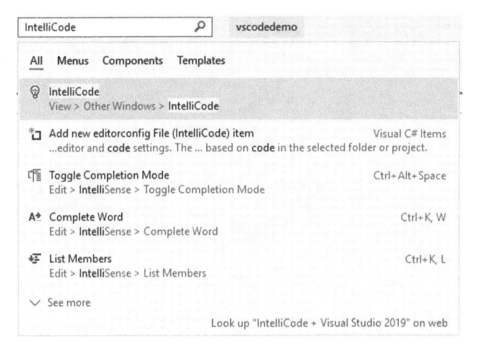

Figure 6-67. *Search for and open IntelliCode window*

Once the IntelliCode window is open (Figure 6-68), you will notice that no models have been trained for the current solution. What training does is it analyzes your code, uploads your metadata to the cloud, and learns your code's patterns.

Code analysis happens on your machine and extracts information about your code that gets sent to IntelliCode's model service. It then gets uploaded to the cloud where a model is generated that is sent back to IntelliCode on your machine.

It is important to note that none of your code is ever uploaded to the IntelliCode cloud service. Only metadata is sent to the cloud, so all your source code stays on your machine.

With the custom model generated, IntelliCode can now give you starred recommendations off of your custom classes and types.

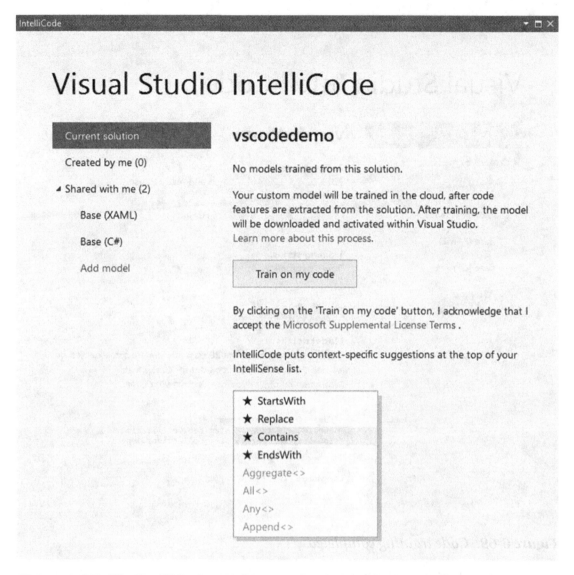

Figure 6-68. *The IntelliCode window*

Depending on the size of your code base, the training process can take a few minutes to complete. Once the training has completed (Figure 6-69), you will see the following information in the IntelliCode window.

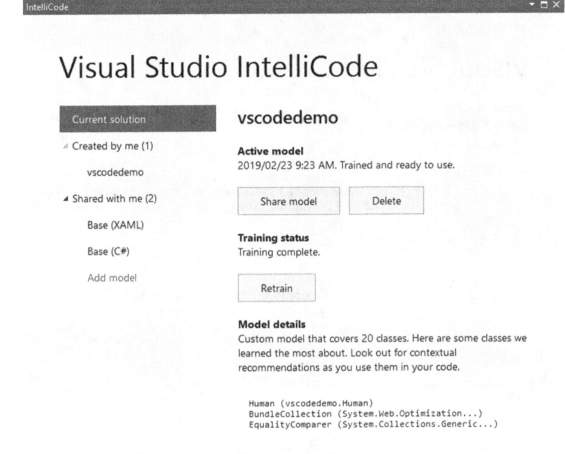

Figure 6-69.   *Code training completed*

The date is displayed when the custom model was trained. You can share or delete the model if needs be. You can also retrain your IntelliCode at any time. Another interesting detail is that the IntelliCode window gives you a gist of what was trained in the model details section.

```
Human.PrintPersonInfo("Sally", "Johnson", 32);
fullName = Human.FullName(Human.NameOrder.FirstLast);
fnSplit = fullName.Split(' ');
WriteLine(fnSplit[0]);

Human.PrintPersonInfo("Larry", "Leisure", 27);
fullName = Human.|
```

⊕	★ FullName
🔧	Age
⊕	Equals
🔧	FirstName
⊕	FullName
🔧	LastName
▱	NameOrder
⊕	PrintPersonInfo
⊕	ReferenceEquals

Figure 6-70. *IntelliCode recommendations using the custom model*

Heading back to your code, if you have a look at the starred recommendations, you will see that the FullName method is starred (Figure 6-70). It now knows this because it has analyzed how I write my code and how my classes and types look like.

Microsoft has enabled IntelliCode to work on

- XAML in Visual Studio

- C++ in Visual Studio

- JavaScript/TypeScript in Visual Studio Code

- Java in Visual Studio Code

IntelliCode is an excellent productivity tool that works off of your own code to make you more productive. The power of AI in Visual Studio.

General Visual Studio Tips

Visual Studio offers you so much flexibility in what you can do. It is the gold standard of IDEs in my opinion. As mentioned earlier in this chapter, some of the finer tips and features might get overlooked. This is especially true in the fast-paced industry we work in. The following tips are not specific to Visual Studio 2019 (even though some details surrounding the feature I expand on might be) and provide a lot of value to developers.

Using Live Unit Tests

Unit tests are actually quite essential in your code. Using unit tests can ensure that the code you write continues to work as you change and improve your code. The reason it is called unit testing is because you break up and test smaller portions of your code as individual units.

The benefits of unit tests can therefore be defined as follows:

- Protect against regression (as your code changes)

- View method outcomes (executable documentation)

- Unit tests force you to decouple your code

Visual Studio contains Test Explorer, a window from which you can view the results of your unit tests and run failed tests again.

When we talk about decoupling code, we mean to say that if your test is complex or difficult to write, simplify the code being tested.

The characteristics of a unit test that adds value to your code are as follows:

- The tests will run fast, even in big projects.

- Your tests should be able to be run in isolation, without any external dependencies such as files or databases.

- You can run the same test multiple times, and if you don't change any code, return the same result.

There are of course many other aspects to unit tests, but that can fill a book on its own. Let us see the use of unit tests in some simple code using Visual Studio. Consider the following code listing.

Listing 6-5. Method to test

```
public static void PrintDate(string date)
{
    WriteLine($"The date is {date}");
}
```

As you can see, all that this method does is print out the date passed to this method to a console window.

Consider the possibility that you need to ensure that the date is in a specific format before printing it out to the console window.

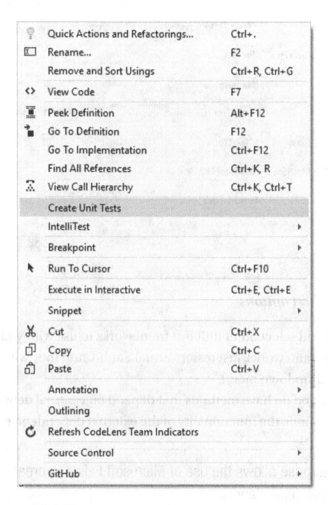

Figure 6-71. *Create Unit Tests*

For this, we can create a unit test by right-clicking the method and selecting *Create Unit Tests* from the context menu (Figure 6-71).

Visual Studio will then display a dialog window (Figure 6-72) where you can configure the unit tests being created. In the following example, you will see that I am using MSTestv2 as the test framework.

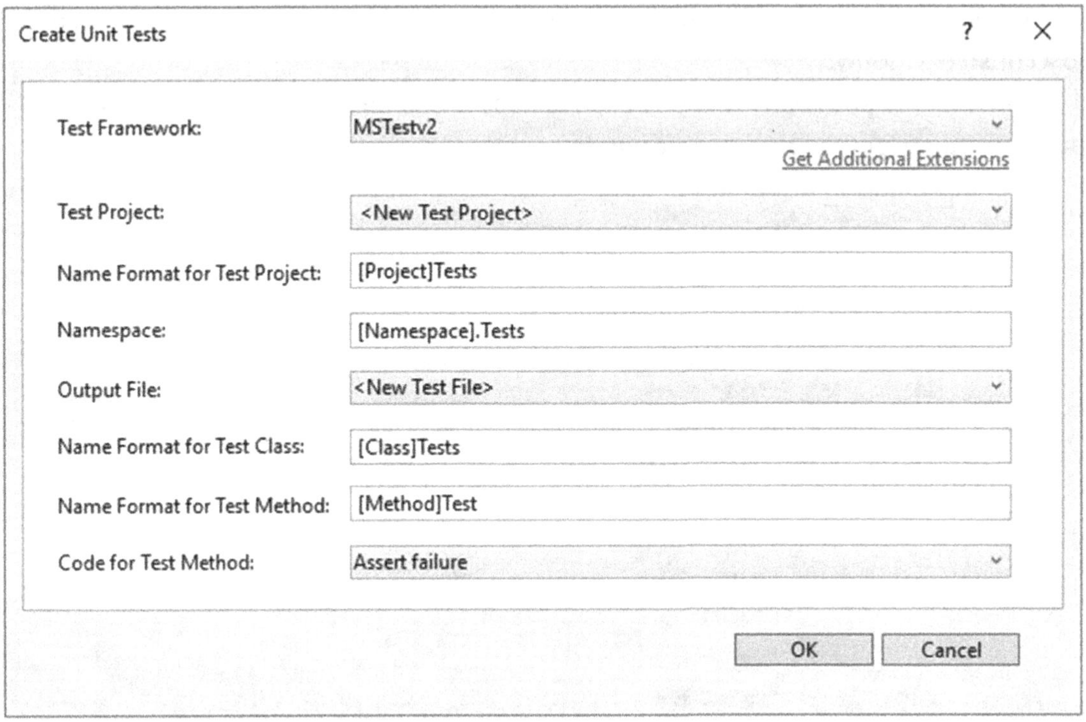

Figure 6-72. *Unit test options*

You can install and select other unit test frameworks to use with your unit tests. After installing the other frameworks, just restart Visual Studio, and they will be available for selection from the dropdown menu.

Also note that if you do have methods that depend on external dependencies, you can create stubs to mimic the functionality of the external dependencies.

Visual Studio Enterprise allows the use of Microsoft Fakes to create substitute classes for external dependencies.

When you have configured your unit test properties, click the OK button. This will create a new test project in your Solution Explorer as seen in Figure 6-73.

Figure 6-73. *Test project created*

You will notice that you now have some boilerplate code added for you that includes the method you wanted to test.

Listing 6-6. Created Test Class

```
[TestClass()]
public class ProgramTests
{
    [TestMethod()]
    public void PrintDate ()
    {
        Assert.Fail();
    }
}
```

As you iterate through your code base, you can expand on the test methods you create and change the code being tested.

The code being tested in the PrintDate method is not complex at all, and you would definitely expand more on the test method than simply leaving the Assert.Fail in there.

It is here that you would generally be able to determine if the code being tested is too complex or too tightly coupled. You are then able to simplify the method being tested, and then you should find it easier to create unit tests for your code.

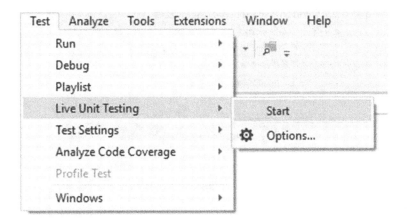

Figure 6-74. *Start Live Unit Testing*

Visual Studio includes the *Live Unit Testing* feature that allows you to run your tests in the background. This means that test results are presented to you in real time as you change and add to your code (Figure 6-74).

If you add additional code (a new method, for example), Visual Studio will notify you if the method is covered by a unit test. This acts as a nice reminder to write unit tests as you go along.

You can configure the general settings for Live Unit Tests by going to *Tools* ➤ *Options* ➤ *Live Unit Testing* ➤ *General*. Here you are able to cap the memory usage used for Live Unit Testing, define the maximum number of test processes, enter a timeout value for test cases, and so on.

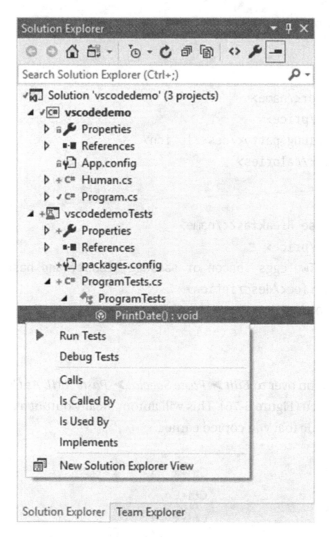

Figure 6-75. *Run tests from Solution Explorer in VS2019*

As of Visual Studio 2019, you can now run unit tests right from within the Solution Explorer as can be seen in Figure 6-75. This is really a solid addition to Visual Studio, as it gives you more flexibility when running your tests.

Generate Classes from XML and JSON

Another often overlooked feature of Visual Studio is creating classes from XML or JSON code. This means that you can copy the following XML (for example) and paste it as a class that Visual Studio creates.

Listing 6-7. Sample XML

```xml
<restaurant>
  <food>
    <name>Hamburger</name>
    <price>$5.95</price>
    <description>160g patty</description>
    <calories>875</calories>
  </food>
  <food>
    <name>Farmhouse Breakfast</name>
    <price>$6.95</price>
    <description>Two eggs, bacon or sausage, toast, and hash brown.
    Bottomless coffee</description>
    <calories>820</calories>
  </food>
</restaurant>
```

To do this, head on over to *Edit* ➤ *Paste Special* ➤ *Paste XML As Classes* or *Paste JSON As Classes* menu (Figure 6-76). This will automatically output a class that maps to the XML or JSON code that you copied earlier.

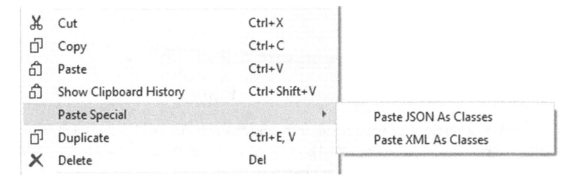

Figure 6-76. *Paste Special*

This is a fantastic time saver for anyone working with a lot of XML or JSON. Here's looking at you again SYSPRO developers.

C# Interactive

How many times have you been in the middle of writing code that isn't quite ready to run, but you really need to test some functionality? It can be a pain commenting out code just to test a small portion of it. It is also a pain to start a full debug session, especially when you are working on a web application with a login page and the bit of code you want to test is in a submenu a few levels deep. Debug that five times.

The world seems a little less bright after the first few iterations of logging in, navigating to the page you need to debug, and waiting for the breakpoint to hit. Combine this with a bit of a lengthy compile and you have a recipe for some frustration.

This is where C# Interactive really shines. Assume that I have some small bit of code that I want debugged. Consider the example in Figure 6-77.

```
var someText = "The rain falls mainly on the plain in Spain";
var arrWords = someText.Split(' ');
var newText = "";
foreach (var word in arrWords)
{
    var textToAppend = word.Equals("mainly") ? "gently" : word;
    newText += word;
}

WriteLine(newText);
```

Figure 6-77. *Some code to test*

The code is not complex, but I want to make sure that my code is rewriting the string correctly to read *gently* instead of *mainly*.

Select the code you want to run, right-click it, and click *Execute in Interactive* from the context menu (Figure 6-78).

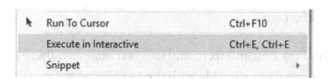

Figure 6-78. *Execute in Interactive*

You can also hold down *Ctrl+E, Ctrl+E* to do the same thing.

The code that you selected will be displayed in the C# Interactive window as seen in Figure 6-79 and will be run to produce the output from that.

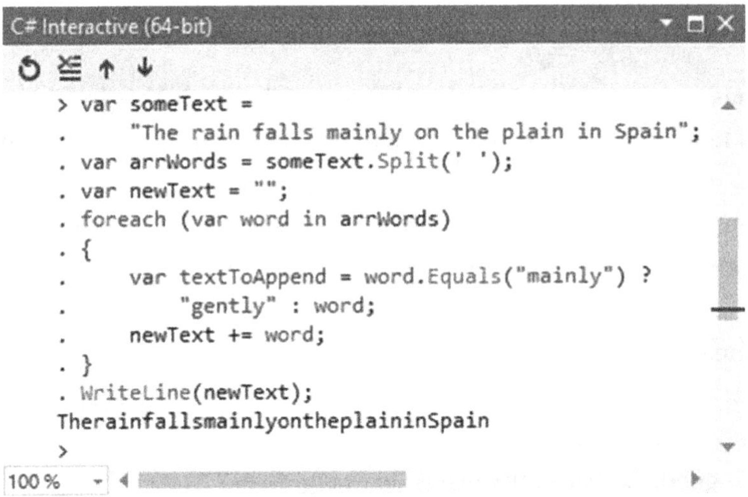

Figure 6-79. *C# Interactive*

As you can see, I have a bug in my code. The word *mainly* is not being replaced and there are no spaces in my text.

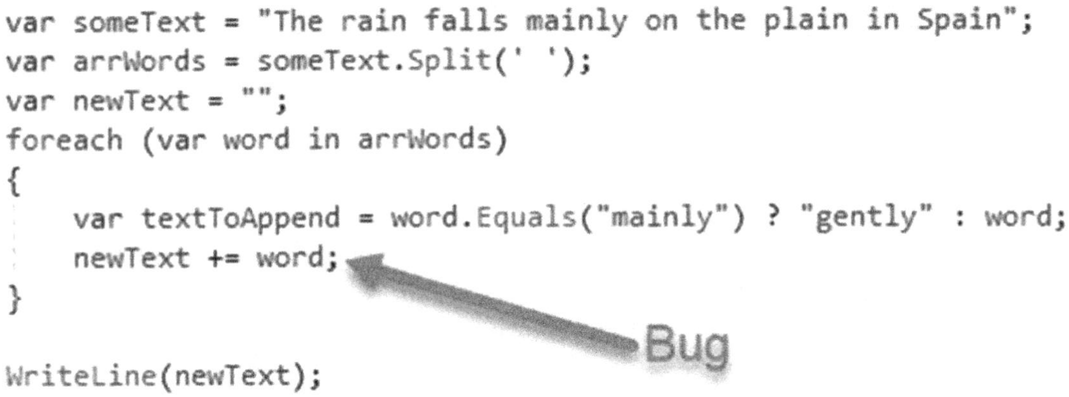

```
var someText = "The rain falls mainly on the plain in Spain";
var arrWords = someText.Split(' ');
var newText = "";
foreach (var word in arrWords)
{
    var textToAppend = word.Equals("mainly") ? "gently" : word;
    newText += word;
}

WriteLine(newText);
```

Figure 6-80. *Find the bug*

I now need to find my bug and fix it, and can you believe... there it is (Figure 6-80). I forgot to append the newText variable with the textToAppend variable value. I need to rewrite my line of code to look as follows: newText += $"{textToAppend} ";

Making the code fix is quick and I can then run the code again in C# Interactive to check that it works correctly (Figure 6-81): https://docs.microsoft.com/en-us/visualstudio/ide/using-intellisense?view=vs-2017.

```
C# Interactive (64-bit)                              ▼ ▫ ✕

⟳ ≊ ↑ ↓

  > var someText =
  .     "The rain falls mainly on the plain in Spain";
  . var arrWords = someText.Split(' ');
  . var newText = "";
  . foreach (var word in arrWords)
  . {
  .     var textToAppend = word.Equals("mainly") ?
  .         "gently" : word;
  .     newText += $"{textToAppend} ";
  . }
  . WriteLine(newText);
  The rain falls gently on the plain in Spain
  > |

100 %   ▼ ◀ ▓▓▓▓▓▓▓▓▓▓▓▓▓▓▓▓▓▓▓▓▓▓              ▶
```

Figure 6-81. *Testing the bug fix*

This time, the output is what I expect.

There are better ways to write this logic, but I'm just illustrating a point here.

C# Interactive is a debugging tool that allows for fast, iterative code runs without you needing to resort to a full debug session just to test a small portion of code.

Wrapping Up

Visual Studio is a feature-rich IDE, there is no doubt about that. I could go on forever and a day about the tips and tricks, features, and gems in Visual Studio. In this chapter we had a look at the new features available to developers in Visual Studio 2019.

We discussed Visual Studio Live Share and saw how we could collaborate on a project on different IDEs and different platforms. We saw how to perform some useful refactorings and code fixes. Then we looked at how we could define the style rules for our code and export these to an *.editorconfig* file. We also saw how Visual Studio IntelliCode brings the power of AI to developers.

The release of Visual Studio 2019 brings more productivity features to the developer's toolbelt. We are able to write code quicker and more accurately. We can collaborate with our team members easier and express our intent clearer. The future looks really bright for developers, and Visual Studio makes it shine even brighter.

Index

W, X, Y, Z